Manchester...
The Sinister Side

CRIME AND THE CAUSES OF CRIME

INTRODUCTION

'If you say in any other part of England that you are from Manchester you are at once supposed to be a thief' (W.B.Neale 1840).

From 1840 onwards, particularly the next fifty years, the city's reputation, if anything, got worse. This was in part due to the flight of the wealthy classes to the suburbs, but the dehumanising living conditions of those left behind further contributed to Manchester's descent into squalor and crime.

Large families were forced to live in damp, overcrowded rooms, where disease was rife and the life-expectancy of infants below the age of twelve months, amongst the worst in the country.

Both men and women, on low incomes, sought temporary relief from the bestial filthiness of their homes and workplaces, by pickling their brains with copious amounts of beer and gin. Troublesome children would be treated with a dose of laudanum.

Drink was a contributory factor in the many cases of wife-beating and assault that came before the beak. It was a common sight to witness heavily-bandaged women testifying against brutish husbands. Most, however, simply suffered in silence.

Life was particularly harsh for women. They were poorly paid, barred from many professions and often dependent on men in and out of work, many of whom preferred to hand their money over to publicans than the family purse. Given the choice between the long hours and hard graft of domestic servitude, factory work or life on the streets, thousands of women turned to prostitution to make ends meet.

Join us for a journey to the grim realities of life, from the birth of the City (1853) to the true end of Victorian values (1914), in *Manchester... the Sinister Side.*

First published in 1997 by
Wicked Publications
222, Highbury Road, Bulwell,
Nottingham NG6 9FE, England
Telephone: (0115) 975 6828

By the same author:

LONDON... THE SINISTER SIDE

WICKED LONDON

LONDON THROUGH THE KEYHOLE

CAPITAL PUNISHMENTS

IN DARKEST LONDON

WHEN THE LIGHTS WENT DOWN

NOTTINGHAM... THE SINISTER SIDE

see back pages for details

Typeset and printed in Great Britain by:
DESA Ltd.,
Forest Mills, Alfreton Road, Nottingham.

CONTENTS

'ONE MASS OF PROSTITUTE, THIEF AND FOOL'

Forget romanticised Christmas cards depicting happy Victorian families singing carols in the snow. Life, for all but extremely wealthy Mancunians, consisted of very long working hours, followed by brief moments of 'leisure' in damp, overcrowded slums, vile beyond description.

In 1854 the Inspector of Common Lodging Houses published details as to how home conditions must have been for many of the impoverished inhabitants of Salford:

In the cellar of 53, Silk street were Mary Kernon, her son aged 20, daughter aged 17, in a bed on the floor. Thomas Hammond, aged 18, was in a second bed in the same cellar. Arthur Anderson, his wife and four children, Jane 17, May 14, Theresa 12 and Henry 9, were sleeping on the floor in the front cellar.

In the cellar of 31, Barrow street were 18 persons:- Catherine Cooley and child 2 years old in the first bed, Maria McCall and three children – Mary 12, John 11 and Patrick 8, in the same bed on the floor; Sarah Henley and three children Maria 11, Patrick 9, (third child not named). Sleeping on the floor in the back cellar; Thomas Andrews, his wife and six children: Mary 16, Ellen 14, Amelia 12, James 10, Bridget 9, Robert 5 on the floor in two beds of shavings.

The Deansgate area was synonymous with dirt, disease and depravity from as far back as 1832, as described by Dr. James Kay:-

A mass of buildings inhabited by prostitutes and thieves. [It] is intersected by narrow and loathsome streets, and close courts defiled with refuse. In Parliament Street there is only one privy for 380 inhabitants which is placed in a narrow passage whence its effluvia infest the adjacent houses, and must prove a fertile source of disease. In this Street also, cesspools with open grids have been made close to the doors of the houses, in which disgusting refuse accumulates and whence its noxious effluvia constantly exhale.

1. A group of male paupers. The uniform at the workhouse consisted of a corduroy suit with waistcoats and belts and a knotted red spotted handkerchief. Whiskers, walking-sticks, hobnailed boots and a miserable demeanour appear to have been in vogue.

2. *It would still be a very long time before the children had running water or a nutritious diet.*

Not only was Deansgate infamous for its squalor and seediness, it was also a hotbed of crime. Alfred Alsop, the young superintendent of a mission house, pulled no punches in his description of a *Deansgate Street* published c1876:

Robberies, acts of violence, the darkest of crimes – even to murder itself – have been committed. Twelve years ago, in broad daylight it was unsafe for a stranger to go down alone; and now, when the shades of evening fall no stranger goes down unmolested. Upon every side are to be found houses whose occupiers are returned convicts, sharpers, smashers, thieves, harlots, gaol-birds, fortune-tellers, unlicensed retailers of beer – all of whom are well known to the police. Their looks are demoniac – their language steeped in blasphemy – the very air is polluted by their horrid curses – their actions lazy, brutal, cowardly, drunken, demoralising – their morals are at the lowest possible strata. The very scum of the city, the very essence of hell, seems to be concentrated here.

SALFORD LOW LIFE

A similar scenario could be found just across the Irwell towards the end of the century:

Crompton Street was one standard poor. Lyme Street was, oh it was awful, much lower than normal. They were living under a horrible condition. Broken windows. Really you couldn't believe the difference in two streets. Mixed up with Jews and thieves. Crompton Street they weren't too bad... They were very hard worked anyway. They didn't all work in Lyme Street... They lived like chip choppers... chopping chips and selling them in bundles – firewood... children going round with them. They were a better type of people in Crompton Street. Although as I say there was a criminal opposite to us.

A family named O'Brien had the first house in Lyme Street... He was a high-class tailor. They hadn't a stick in the house... Nice man, Mr. O'Brien. Their children were no good. And the mother... used to take several policemen to lock her up and they always had to take her on a hand cart. That was Lyme Street. And O'Brien the poor fellow, he put up with it.

According to one, somewhat circumspect witness, the Stacey family were the real low life:

Everybody knew them. They were downright villains. They were thieves. The women were bad women, really bad women. One eloped with a doctor. The doctor must have been mad. And they were barmaids some of them till they got a bit older and then they went to lob. Went to bed. Lob – made love.

The eldest son, I think it was Paddy, he was always in and out of prison. Violence and drunkenness... He died from head injuries in the prison... saw him one day in Chapel Street, walking drunk, talking to himself with a brick in his hand. He used to throw bricks through pub windows... I saw another criminal drop dead out of a pub. Paddy Talman. He was a villain... He lived off Blackgate, married to a fine young woman and I was coming home from work and I saw this fellow. I'd a bit of

truckle with him once, I was glad they'd got rid of him... Doctor came, he was dead, shot through the heart. Now what had happened – the publican had raised a stool up to hit him and this revolver – well he might have done, I don't know. But there was one of the Stacey girls mixed up with him in the pub in that.

Joe Toole, another Salfordian, remembered the near impossibility of feeding eleven mouths on a weekly wage of 19 shillings:

Unfortunately immediately the nineteen shillings arrived on Saturdays, there were so many 'additional

3. St. Mary's and Deansgate in the 1870s . Boy's suits 8s. 6d. Celebrated trousers 16s. from Beaty Bros. Clothes were often the main target of thieves, especially women.

arrivals', chief among whom was the landlord. He took six shillings away every week. When he had gone the insurance man was in evidence for it is a hard custom in all the industrial parts of Britain that immediately a child arrives in the world provision must be made for its passing to the next world... When the aforesaid payments had been made, there was often a call from the hire-purchase man who supplied trashy timber, highly-polished as high-class furniture, and last, but by no means least, never an irregular caller, would be the clothing-club man, who, for two shillings per week, would supply the whole family with new suits and frocks...

Every new home in Salford seemed to be the same – no bath and no sanitary arrangements as we know them now, but it appeared general that each family should hang upon the walls of their home a picture, the cheapest obtainable. The most popular were 'Daniel in the Den of Lions' and 'Moses in the Bulrushes.'

JOURNEY INTO THE UNKNOWN

In the early 1870s two reporters, determined to reveal the true brutish facts of existence experienced by the majority of Mancunians, sallied forth into the slums.

The correspondent from the *Manchester Evening*

4. Deansgate in the 1870s. "Upon every side are to be found houses whose occupants are returned convicts, sharpers, smashers, thieves, warlords, gaol-birds, fortune-tellers, unlicensed retailers of beer – all of whom are known to the police".

News was intrigued by the operations of the criminal underworld. During his investigation he met and heard tales of the city's most infamous characters, including 'Fat Billy', 'Big Jack', 'Johnny the Kid', 'Fat Ann', 'Liza Lanky', 'one-armed Kitty', 'Aunty Mary', 'Cockney Charlie', 'Ginger Liz', and the two cabbages – 'Cabbage Kate' and 'Cabbage Ann'. (The derivation of these nicknames is fairly obvious, though the meaning of `cabbage', in this context, is less certain. There is no record of the girls' feelings on the subject.) Most of the above worked as fences but were willing to turn their hands to any new scam for the sake of a few pence.

Nearly all the poorer classes, outside workhouses, rented rooms in sodden slums or common lodging-houses. One of the better ones was to be found in Charter Street, here described by the *Guardian* reporter:

Here are the traces of wet streaming through innumerable places in the roof. Beds are placed foot to foot, so as to touch each other. The attic ceiling is black with damp and decay. Doors are torn from their hinges... It is all free fighting here: even some of the windows do not open so it is useless to cry for help.

Further evidence of the neglect by owners of

5. *The King's Arms c 1870, at the junction of King Street and Deansgate (pre-widening). The young Reverend Alsop wrote of life in the area at this time: "On the average we have, the year round, four free fights day and night, some being of a murderous nature".*

rental properties was found in Angel Street, where the walls in some houses were so saturated that plaster would not hang. In Deansgate a couple took to their bed in the kitchen. The only bedding they possessed was an old black and broken straw palisse with just one rag to cover them, the rain having flowed through the roof saturating all floors and ceilings. They could not afford to light a fire and there was not a scrap of food in the house. They were forced into the kitchen, this being the driest room in the house. From the evidence of the soot and water-stained kitchen ceiling the rain would soon be seeping through. The reporters silently stole away, leaving the couple shivering and cuddling each other for some vestiges of warmth, hoping against hope that the rain would cease.

NO PRIVACY IN THE PRIVIES

Hunger and cold were not the only hardships endured by the majority of Mancunians. The overpowering stench of refuse and human waste pervaded whole areas of the inner city. In Olive Street conditions were extremely overcrowded and unsavoury. For every ten or twelve properties housing some 200 people, there was only one privy – an ashpit about four feet square – without a door and rarely, if ever, cleaned.

Near Nelson Street the *Guardian* reporter stumbled across:

…an open space covered with filth and reeking with foul smells – a place which a woman whose house abuts upon it avers 'has never been cleaned since she knowed it'. It's pretty decent now, she says and she can let her front room off, the which as times are bad she is glad to do; but in summer time she cannot do this as the stench from the filth deposit is so dreadful she cannot live in the back part of the house and is obliged to occupy the front herself.

At the end of Back-Irk street another woman shared a similar problem. Here one inhabitant was reluctant to remove the ashes from the grate as all the filth followed and the house was 'redolent of stinks'.

Near Style Street the privies were not cleaned for years on end. Our intrepid *Guardian* investigator had the unenviable job of reporting from the scene:

In the half-dark places are four privies in such a condition that it is almost impossible to enter them. The floor is a flood of urine and a puss of ordure. The ashpit is overflowing with decaying vegetable refuse…

Having witnessed the deprivations and hardships of home life, was there any escape at work? In the tailoring sweatshops the answer was a definite 'no' – if anything, the conditions were even worse.

In 1888 a reporter from *The Lancet* visited 146 tailors in Manchester. He discovered that their pay had not risen from 6d. per hour for over twenty years and, in workshops without unions, was often less. He was, however, more interested in the physical conditions at work, including the provision of toilet facilities, than the rates of pay. He found many sweatshops to be 'of the worst and filthiest kind'. Following is his description of a Jewish sweathouse in the Strangeways area:

The ceiling was black with soot, and at one end there was a huge pile of dust, dirt and scraps of cloth, which was about three feet wide, twelve feet long and sixteen inches deep. There were twelve men and women working here, and eight in the garret above the stable. Both these workshops had access to a closet in the yard, which was also used by the stablemen and by five people inhabiting a house joining on the same yard.

At the lowest computation thirty persons used this one closet and when work is brisk the number must be much greater. Under such circumstances, we were not surprised to find the closet in a filthy condition, with soil on the seat.

In two other sweatshops conditions were even worse:

At the time of our visit nine persons were busily engaged sorting rags. They receive 6s. a week pay, and are themselves dressed in tatters. We saw fragments of dirty old clothes sorted, the better pieces of cloth torn off, each operation creating a cloud of dust. In the yard there was one closet, locked up, the key being kept by the tailor above, so that the rag-sorters had no closet. In answer to our question they stated they went to a private house in a neighbouring street, but judging from the filth in the yard, it was very evident they did not always take that trouble. By the side of the closed closet door, in a little wooden recess, there was a rusty broken, iron urinal, and on the ground a heap of faecal matter and pools of urine formed in indentures of the black earth.

A great portion of the remaining part of the yard was covered with refuse of every description, broken bottles, brickbats, cinders, pieces of cloth, rags, paper, old shoes &c.

Above one of the tailors' workshops is a cloth cap manufactory, where forty, sometimes fifty persons, for the most part young girls, are employed. These all use one single closet placed under the stairs, on the same level as the tailors' workshop, from which the closet is only separated by a wooden partition. Consequently, and especially during the summer, the tailors are invaded either by evil odours or an overpowering smell of disinfectants.

6. No. 40 Deansgate, near Bridge Street. An excellent photo for the 1870s well worth a more detailed examination with a magnifying glass. There was no doubt as to the main pastime those days!

The top hat made its first appearance in London in 1797 and immediately became a target for rotting vegetables. It was common in all walks of life in the 1870s.

Some people went to public houses to spend a penny, but with little privacy in the privies, many simply downed their drawers in the streets.

Not far from Crown Lane could be found:

…a recess in the open street, and off this open space, in full view of all the passers-by, we find the privies and ashpits of the neighbourhood. The houses here have no back yards, and as a consequence, all those domestic operations usually performed in the privacy of these enclosures are necessarily carried on in public view, and the state of the street is most disgustingly filthy; animal and vegetable refuse lie there, rotting, festering and fever-breeding, and the public way is the receptacle for the contents of the night-pail and washtub. The ashpit walls are broken down and the contents overflow into the open space; and the stench, even in the hard frost, is sickening.

7. Mary Scully, like many prostitutes had letters tattooed onto her arm.

WORK, THE CURSE OF THE DRINKING CLASSES

Some people chose to work from home. As today, these were the most exploited. With life being one long drudge it is not surprising that some sought escape in the bottle, and who could blame them?

Their homes were in some instances of microscopic dimensions, and the surroundings unsuitable in the extreme. Here and there they were only cellar dwellings. One room measured nine feet by ten feet four inches. The ceiling and floor were giving way, and covered with soot and dirt; and yet here a man and his wife slept, cooked their meals and made clothes.

In another similar house our inquiries were somewhat baffled by the fact that both the tailor and tailoress present had been indulging so freely in Easter activities that they failed to understand the motive of our visit. Seeing the misery of their home and surroundings, we could scarcely be surprised at their seeking forgetfulness in dissipations which even those who are well educated and wealthy cannot always resist.

Finally another home worker slept and worked in a little room surrounded by a numerous family, where the damp was causing the plaster to fall off the walls and the door was broken in. In the back yard the drainage seemed out of order; damp, wet and unpleasant odours prevailed.

To both physically and mentally escape the filthy conditions that surrounded them, men and women spent whatever spare time and cash they could muster in their local. With conditions being as they were, and pubs open for up to 21 hours a day – typically from 4.a.m. to 1.a.m. – it was inevitable some ale houses would degenerate into dens of depravity. Amongst the most notorious were the 'Dog and Rat' the 'Old Ship', the 'Red, White and Blue' and the 'Green Man'.

In Chapel Street, popping out to spend a penny may have had an alternative connotation in the Butcher's Arms, which doubled up as a brothel. Samuel Hancock, the licensee, was charged with keeping a disorderly house and fined £5. Investigators found a number of rooms full of couches and pillows with fastenings inside the doors. Three notorious prostitutes were in permanent residence.

There were many streets in contention for boasting the worst dens of vice, but Wood Street, Calhoun Street and Richmond Street would have been co-favourites. Pubs in these areas attracted

8. *Fanny Butterworth, known to her friends and customers alike as 'Skemming Fanny'. A hard-headed hard-drinking prostitute and thief. Not to be crossed!*

the dregs and sweepings of the underworld who engaged in drinking and brawling in licentious revelry.

The 'Old Cat's Face' in Market Street, despite having lost its licence, was another mecca for low life:

It is crowded with dirty drunkards – too dirty and too drunkard to be admitted into any public-house desirous of retaining the legal right to make men 'drunk on the premises'. The majority of the creatures here are low thieves who find this a safer rendezvous than the more open public-house, and who are content to pay a trifle more for their beer as the price of additional security.

No evening's entertainment was complete without a good bout of fisticuffs and in the 1870s Deansgate was the rendezvous for the city's prize fighters. Well-known pugilists slugged each other senseless in the cellars of public-houses or in garrets. Many of the houses kept a full-sized ring with stakes and ropes ready for any fistically enhanced customer who wanted it and large sums

of money changed hands. By way of variety, dogs would be trained to savage each other in the name of sport for the entertainment of a drunken, bloodthirsty gathering of 'sports lovers'.

Missionary Alsop, like most men of the cloth inclined to exaggerate a tad, kept a diary of what he personally witnessed:

5.p.m. Wednesday – Loud shouts; stones, pieces of house slating, bricks, flying about in all directions; but the principal actor is a big strong cattle drover, with high boots and leather leggings, most unmercifully kicking a poor young woman, at the same time tearing handsful of hair off her head; for a moment she gets loose, when, exasperated beyond all endurance, she rushes at him with the half of a slate, aiming direct for his head, which, had it fallen, would have cleaved it open. The writer, who got bedaubed with blood, seized him; the woman was dragged into a house, the police then came; and the immense crowd separated at the usual "Move on there."

3.30.p.m. Friday – Some poor girls had been indulging freely in the drink, when a fight began and resulted in one of them biting off a portion of the other girl's ear, for which cannibalism she was sentenced to three months' hard labour.

12 to 1 Monday – On some spare ground, where once stood the notorious Old Ship, were some score of men and women, eyes blazing with passion, and fighting furiously. Stones, bricks, fists, belts and clogs were unsparingly used – flesh torn, blood flowing, hair pulled out by the roots. Such was the picture for about twenty minutes.

Whereas men sought some brief escape from their harsh lives by pickling their brains, a little sport and a short squalid sexual encounter, women's sole release seemed to be found in the gin houses and pubs. For some, the more squalid the more they felt at home. Even when pubs lost their licence many carried on trading. One of the most notorious was the 'Up the Sough' on Whittle Street where our *Guardian* reporter found:

Men and women, quite drunk and half clad, sitting and lying about in all directions. Of liquors, albeit there was no licence, there was no lack. Some of the occupants of this den were quarrelling, some were singing ribald songs, and all the wretchedness of vicious intoxication was rampant and unchecked. We have seen a good deal of vice and villainy but the scenes which we saw 'Up the Sough' have burned themselves in our memory so strongly, that they stand out prominently amongst the many other pictures of misery we have seen in the 'slums'.

Name *Elizabeth*
Alias "
Trade *Prostitute*
Where born *Blackburn*
Last Residence *Rochdale*
Age *26 years in 1892*
Height *5ft 4 inches*
Complexion *Fresh*
Eyes *Grey*   Hair, *Brown*
Marks

Name *Mary*
Alias *Jane*
Trade *Prostitute*
Where born *Stockport*
Last Residence *Rochdale*
Age *25 years*
Height *5ft 3 inches*
Complexion *Sallow*
Eyes *black*   Hair *black*.
Marks

Name *Ada*
Alias
Trade *Prostitute*
Where born *Rochdale*
Last Residence "
Age *18 years in 1893*
Height *4ft 11 inches*
Complexion *Fresh*
Eyes *blue*   Hair *brown*
Marks *None*.

9. Three ladies of the night. Although their trade might be listed as 'prostitute' most girls were convicted for stealing clothes and money or being drunk and disorderly. Elizabeth was familiar with Strangeways having been convicted 30 times. Mary would steal anything not nailed down, including clothes from clothes lines. Ada was sent to prison for two weeks for stealing 2s. 6d.

Near Butterworth's Court the *M.E.N* reporter came across a house where:

...a girl of 18 years of age was lying dead-drunk across two chairs. Her feet touched the ground at one end of this hard bed, and her head was hanging down, with her hair streaming on to the bricks, at the other. Several women were in the same place with two or three children, but they took the whole business as a matter of course, and went on with their supper as if drunkenness was nothing more than an every-day occurrence.

What might loosely be described as 'music' emanated from many of the drinking establishments. Mechanical organs, drums and tambourines, as well as the ubiquitous joanna, were played with varying degrees of skill. The singing was not always in tune as one drunkard confided to the *Guardian* correspondent: *Anything is good enough for a drunken man but this is almost too bad for that.*

Let's join our *M.E.N.* man in one of the unlicensed public houses:

In Wood-street we were arrested by the sound of music proceeding from what looked like an old beer-house, and on entering we came upon a party of a dozen youths and girls assembled in a half-furnished room, which resembled a taproom, listening to a 'hurdy-gurdy' man grinding out a lugubrious waltz and a red-faced girl, with a glaring red shawl over her shoulders shaking a tambourine.

The audience was a small one, but there was enough dirt and old clothes among them to stock a marine-store dealer. They were altogether more disreputable-looking than the denizens of Charter-street; the women were all bareheaded, save the strata of cheap oil and the dust of weeks which covered their hair, and the men were in a chronic state of tight-fitting cloth caps and large parti-coloured mufflers.

10. Not all were found guilty. The lovely Elizabeth Reynolds was acquitted of the charge of 'being a suspicious character' at the January sessions of 1873. An early photo certain to interest followers of fashion.

11. Newgates, Corporation Street 1908 where even the washing wasn't safe. Note the water tap and privies for the whole street. Newgates backed on to Pearsons Court.

Many of the songs unashamedly advocated the life of crime adopted by so many. The following lyrics, sung in a shrill treble by a young lad, gives a good example of this:

Oh I'm a bloke what gets my livin'
By taking things what isn't given
With my hand, with my fist,
With my juke, with my mauler.
I wish there were no bobbies!
I do! I do!
For the treadmill
It does make me ill;
And I only steals, my belly to fill,
With my hand, with my fist,
With my juke, with my mauler,
(chorus) Oh downy on the blue 'uns.

NOT AT ALL DECOLLETEES

Eric the Red was not the first Frenchman to stay in Manchester. Between 1860 and 1870 Hippolyte Taine, an historian, visited the city. He was interested in how the majority of the people lived and probably came out with a few 'oohs' and 'aahs' when visiting the workhouses, factories, slums and drinking establishments in his quest to uncover the 'real' England. Taine went to Belle Vue one evening to see how the locals spent their leisure. He described the place as:

…a sort of dance casino surrounded by a garden, with stage shows, curiosities and works of trumpery art… Among the flower-beds parties of working-people and small shopkeepers or others of that class sat eating, drinking and playing a game which involved kissing. Inside the building in an enormous room, working men and their girls were dancing, taking big jumps, rather violent but not indecent.

It costs a shilling to go in; sixpence extra for the dance hall. As Belle Vue is quite far out, at the extremity of a suburb, one must add to that the cost of getting here: there was a great number of omnibuses and cabs standing at the door. Add to that again the price of refreshments, and remember

Page 16 and 17 picture: 12.1-13 Pearsons Court 30.6.1908. For family historians, the three girls are probably the daughters of Thomas Heap and the man in the doorway, is Allan France.

that as a rule the workmen that come here bring their 'sweethearts' or a prostitute, and must pay therefore for two. Now a cotton-spinner in a factory earns 23 shillings per week. Here then a good example of English spendthrift ways.

In conversation later that evening, two detectives described to Taine the lives of the majority of workers. According to them, the men married young, at about 18; earned, with their wives as factory hands, around 30 shillings per week; had an average of six children; drank a lot; hardly saved anything and did not leave enough to pay for their own funerals.

Accompanied by the two detectives, Taine set off into the Manchester night to visit a lodging house, a casino and a brothel.

We saw one-night lodgings where, in a low, airless room, there were four or five beds, all occupied: a whole bed cost fivepence, half a bed twopence-ha'penny. One of the beds was occupied by a man and wife: the man's face was a painful sight, haggard with livid patches, the rest yellow, and all lined by sickness, it looked like an old wax mask.

We visited a casino where five hundred people of wretched appearance were crowded on to greasy benches watching a stage where two frail young girls in pink gauze were dancing. The entrance fee was twopence. The audience was drinking gin and smoking, and the air, thick with the emanations of human bodies, was stifling.

Next to a brothel. One of the policemen told us that the girls are recruited chiefly among the mill-girls. They sat in a room downstairs and were not at all decolletees. Several of them were very thin and their ignoble faces had become, as it were, like those of savages. Next to a greasy mulatto woman I noticed a young girl with a pretty delicate, intelligent face, thoughtfully bent towards the red glow of the fire. The month is July but this fire is necessary of an evening. It was the same in thieves' public houses; we saw twenty or thirty of these dens, and there was always a heaped-up fire of red-hot coal to do the cooking and do the washing. The men sit about playing dominoes and smoking; when we came in they said nothing but all raised bright, motionless eyes, the eyes of a beast of prey, and stared at us. The crude gas-light is horrible, playing upon such faces...

Here and there one sees wretched women trailing their faded finery, wearing their professional smile, and as they pass you are tempted to draw away, as from a haunting spectre, a soul in agony... Certainly the vile and horrible are worse in this country than elsewhere.

HALF DRESSED, HALF DRUNK AND REPULSIVE IN THE EXTREME

Many women, not employed in the mills, were forced into one kind of service or another. Some slaved for 18 hours a day cleaning, scrubbing and cooking for tyrannical families little richer than themselves, often forced to fend off the unwanted advances of male members of the household.

Women who, for one reason or another, were not gainfully employed, profited from sexual approaches, selling their bodies to dirty drunkards in darkened alleyways or common lodging houses. In Deansgate alone the police knew of 46 houses of ill-repute but the figure was undeniably much higher.

Where there were brothels there was invariably trouble. Men usually stumbled in and out the worse for wear. They often paid far more than the going rate as most prostitutes were also thieves who had their pimps, or *bullies*, to call on if a punter played up. Once again Alsop, the Lord Longford of 19th Century Manchester, was on hand to witness a typical altercation, when a duped customer tried to retrieve stolen cash:

8.25 p.m., Saturday – A young man of about twenty-two, hailing from the pretty village of Worsley, was tumbled head first out of a notorious brothel; received a blow from a jug on the side of the head, causing a severe wound and blood to flow freely. He had been robbed of several half-crowns, and, upon making the discovery, created a bother in the house – hence his sudden ejectment. We advised him to get quickly away. He cried, bled, roared and caused intense excitement; and begged hard for sixpence to get him home. His good new suit was stained with blood and dirt. After much persuasion he was got away.

Scene in a brothel from the same publication:

11. 45 p.m. Saturday. – Uproar at a brothel. Door broken open, pictures and windows smashed by a rough fellow who had been robbed when inside; someone throws a sharp iron fender; this is laid hold of by the man; he makes a murderous rush at the unfortunate; she screams, drops; he runs, fear giving him speed, and, darkness covering his retreat, he escapes.

KICKING WITH CLOGS IN SALFORD

Punters were at continual risk from prostitutes. Not only might they pick up a dose, there was also the chance they could get a good kicking from a male accomplice or bully. John Coulson certainly got a lot more than he bargained for in the spring of 1874.

William Reeves, 30, and Elizabeth Reeves, 30, were indicted for having, in Salford, on April 21st. assaulted John Coulson, with intent to do him grievous bodily harm. The prosecutor said he was a bacon smoker and lived in Ordsal-lane. About midnight he was going along Chapel-street when he was accosted by the woman who asked him to go home with her. He went with her to 41, Sidmouth street. She asked for some money and while he was putting his hand in his pocket the man rushed in, seized the poker and struck him across the head with it.
Fortunately the witness's hat broke the blow, and he was not much hurt. He ran out into the street, but was followed by the man, who knocked him down, and held him while the woman brought her husband his clogs. Having put them on he kicked the witness two or three times about the head with all his force. Having finished his attacks he went away and the woman then came up, and from her the witness received another blow with the poker.

Having been in gaol on remand for three months prior to trial, the couple were sentenced to only a further three months each.

Prostitutes would keep a special eye out for 'swells', or countrymen new to the city. Plied with alcohol, their pockets picked, these rural rascals would be left to sleep it off, whilst their triumphant hosts moved onto greener pastures, in one or other of Manchester's 2,000 beerhouses. When not 'clocking the countryman' the younger, more attractive girls were seeking 'swells' who worked as clerks in the warehouses. Of a 'cigar shop' in Peter Street the *Guardian* reporter observed:

Behind the shop is a small parlour and behind the parlour a bedroom or even two. There are four females here, well dressed, and alas one's good-looking; but the vile, foul ribaldry and impious blasphemy which reek from their lips are beyond anything we ever heard in Charter-street, and this for the amusement and delectation of a couple of young men, who would be considered swells.

Besides 'swells', successful thieves flush with the fruits of their trade were very much sought after. The principle pick up points were pubs and ginshops, one such, in Oxford Street, being described as *one mass of prostitute, thief and fool.*

Not all girls walked the streets. Eight houses in back-Piccadilly were the destination of men hard up in more ways than one. Their entertainment was definitely at the cheaper end of the market:

The poorer subjects of Her Majesty who are housed here are women – women who are too young, too old or too ugly to carry on their professional avocations for their own pecuniary benefit. They are the slaves of the keepers of these places; the very clothes they wear belong to their masters and mistresses for strange as it may sound, they are owned by both and to them they have to account for all they earn and are watched and spied upon to see that they do not sell themselves. Nothing but the drink they get given to them can they call their own, and we verily believe that this makes them so fond of it.

One house near Canal Street often doubled as a brothel. Here a punter was observed sharing a bottle, in expectation of a group grope, with three doxies.

In the back kitchen, furnished with the customary sofa, table and chairs, far too numerous in proportion to the size of the room, were three women and the inevitable man, in this case an outsider 'on the drunk'. A quart bottle nearly full of dark British brandy, graced the middle of the table, and a drunken, sodden wretch, clad in tawdry finery, with bleared eyes and scrofulous features, was pouring a glass of neat spirit down her throat. She drank the poison without wincing, and helped herself to another, replenishing the glasses of her companions at the same time, for these women can drink with the confidence begotten of long practice, and never dream of spoiling their taste by polluting their mouths with water. Their male 'friend' was subdued and maudlin, but he seemed perfectly content with these Philistines, and glared jealously at us as if expecting we were about to deprive him of the comfort derived from the drunken endearments of these representatives of the gentler sex.

The *M.E.N.* reporter described the prostitutes in the area in the following unflattering manner:

The women are of a class whose degradation is utter, and whose reclamation, as a body, is an absolute impossibility.
The purlieus which hedge about Deansgate afford a shelter to a vice so shameless that it scarcely cares to hide, but obtrudes itself into the public view at the corner of almost every street, and this is unblushingly as though it were miles away from the intense respectability of St. Ann's Square… Devil's gate, not Deansgate, should be the name of the thoroughfare."

Many men spent their hard-earned cash playing away in:

...a public-house filled full to overflowing with wholly drunken men and semi-drunken women, and hard-working labourers are spending on prostitutes hard-earned money, for the want of which their wives and children are starving at home.

Many girls, following in their mother's footsteps, had their first experiences, both alcoholic and sexual, in these so called 'dens of vice'. By the time the *Guardian* reporter was coming to the end of his tour of low life Manchester, he was physically ill and his story takes a turn towards the despair and resignation that must have characterised the lives of his subjects.

Coming across a house in Friday Street he hears a commotion and enters:

It is only a drunken woman who has fallen against the fire-grate, and another drunken woman is trying, but ineffectually, to get her away; so the children scream and we go to the rescue. There's not a scrap of furniture in the room, and one of the drunken women perches herself on the fender and props herself up against the fire-grate, whilst the other lies down on the floor. The most drunken is a visitor, the least drunken the mistress of the house and the mother of seven children. The father is a tailor who 'hasn't come home yet'; what state he will arrive in it is not difficult to anticipate.

Whilst we are endeavouring to prop the woman up in a less suicidal position, two of the daughters come in with flaunting ribbons and rouged cheeks, and they too are drunk. We need not say what their 'ostensible means of gaining a livelihood' is. God help the younger ones; the least seemed about four or five years old, and there was a visible metrical arrangement between the others upwards to the eldest girl of about seventeen. When children grow up amidst such scenes, is it to be wondered at that crime seems high in Manchester? When children fortunately die in such places is it to be wondered at that Manchester is prominently deadly, and that its death-rate is so high as to be a by-word of shame and reproach against us?

SLUMMING IT

In 1888, braving the chill February winds, two members of the 'privileged' classes determined to go slumming it, to visit the interiors of the homes typical of most of Manchester's inhabitants. Openly shocked, Lucretia and her friend revealed their findings to the *Manchester City News*:

Turning off from the great thoroughfare of Oxford Road we soon found ourselves in as different a world as one can imagine from the fashionable parts of the town. Streets with rows of little houses, all of one monotonous pattern, and such courts leading out of those streets – as one has to see – to believe that such places can exist. Swarming with ragged dirty children, and slovenly women gossiping in knots in each other's doors, perfectly regardless of their domestic duties.

Their attention was drawn to a back-to-back house, where five or six women, wrapped in shawls, were conversing in urgent hushed tones. Upstairs a young mother, Jane, was fighting for her life. The two friends entered:

The front room was poorly furnished. A small round deal table, with some tea-things, half a loaf of bread and a piece of very fat bacon on it, stood in the centre. Beside the fire (which was chiefly of cinders), in a wooden arm-chair of an old fashioned straight-backed pattern, sat a labouring man, evidently just come home from his work to a mid-day meal. He never raised his eyes from the fire as we entered and seemed, as it were, dazed with grief. A sickly-looking infant was asleep on a sort of rude sofa under the window. The room was close and oppressive, although the front door was standing open...

We ascended the narrow wooden staircase and entered the squalid bedroom. There on a meagerly-furnished bed, lay a young woman, evidently in the last stage of consumption. Her long dark hair hung down over her shoulders and her bright eye and hectic flush told of the inward consuming fever. Close by to the bedside stood one of the nurses belonging to the Manchester Sick Poor Institution. She was feeding her from a cup with some beef tea.

In a conversation with Jane's mother the familiar sad story of alcohol and wife abuse was revealed:

"Is the master out of work?" I asked.

"Nay," she replied "but he moight as well be: for he gits the drink on a Saturday noight, an' knocks Jane about. Eh! but she doesn't know what I ses" she added, noticing my warning look; "she is past all that poor thing."

I murmured "Dying."

The two 'slummers' left with the nurse whose next call was on another young woman, who had contracted rheumatic fever whilst cleaning doorsteps, her threadbare clothes offering little resistance to the February frosts. As the nurse comforted her the two visitors heard an agonised cry from a nearby house whose door stood open to reveal, once again, the all too familiar tale of child neglect and dire poverty:

13. *Our two female visitors may well have passed along the Rochdale Road during their visit to the slums.*

A ragged little girl about eight came forward on seeing us, and in answer to inquiries said the crying proceeded from her little brother who was very ill; her mother was out at work. We told her we would come in and see if we could do anything for him, and as she seemed so pleased at the idea we entered, and going through the front room came to a sort of kitchen.

Here disorder reigned supreme. No fire was in the grate, although it was a cold damp winter's afternoon; and on the stone floor lay a child about three years old. It appeared unable to move; could neither sit, stand nor crawl. Some intelligence was still existing as he slowly rolled his large black eyes to watch our entrance; the moving of his head seemed a difficulty, and he stretched out his hand eagerly for the biscuit I gave him. The little girl who acted as guide gave me to understand that he usually laid all day on the floor, in the position I found him, whilst the mother went out to work. When she came home from school at noon she fed him, and then he was left alone in the house till four. Sometimes a neighbour would come in and put him straight, and the Sanitary Mission Woman came sometimes, but she was very vexed at finding him laid on the floor, and had gone on 'no end' to her mother for not making him up a little bed. When she

came home she used to nurse him and wash and dress his sores.

"What is the matter with him?"

"Abscesses. Mother takes him when she has time, and gets medicine."

"Does the doctor know he is laid on a cold stone floor all day?"

The child even looked abashed and made no answer.

"Why doesn't your mother put him in a crib or bed?"

"Bed! We ain't got no beds. There ain't nothin' upstairs in the rooms. Father has pawned everything for drink."

"What do you sleep on?"

"We put shawls and cloaks and that on the floor."

A short time later a worker from the sanitary mission arrived to look after the child.

The two friends had seen more than enough of life and death at the sharp end and quietly returned to their lives of comfortable dull domesticity.

Given the above conditions there was no real surprise that man and wife had minor altercations from time to time.

TILL DEATH DO US PART

Fights and confrontations were inevitable in Manchester's squalid slums. Most altercations were between husbands and wives, who set about each other in a drunken frenzy: kicking, biting, scratching and pulling hair.

A middle-aged shoemaker, Patrick Rogers, living at 17, Brown Street off London Road, was brought before the court in the Summer of 1888 charged with assaulting his third wife, Mary. She appeared a sorry figure in court, with both arms and wrists swathed in bandages, her whole body a mass of bruises. She told the court that her husband, dressed *and in his boots* had violently woken her at 6.a.m. demanding one halfpenny. He had obviously got out the wrong side of the bed as, when he was told that she had no money, the incensed husband screamed: *It's now or never. I'll not make two jobs of you.*

Rogers then leapt onto the bed and kicked his poor wife over and over again. It was a full, terrifying 15 minutes before neighbours, hearing the screaming, sobs and pleas, forced an entry. The wife-beater told them that he fully intended to kill Mary and would swing for her because he believed she was seeing another man. He was sentenced to six months with hard labour.

A VITRIOLIC ASSAULT

46-year-old John Mills, however, went a lot further. When his wife found out that he was already married, and therefore a bigamist, she insisted he leave the family home. In retaliation, Mills swore he'd take care of her *as no one else has*. Under the guise of popping out to get some oil for his boots, Mills went shopping. What he bought was not oil but vitriol – concentrated sulphuric acid, which he casually threw into the face of the second Mrs. Mills.

The attack resulted in the loss of Alice Mills's left eye and the complete disfigurement of the face. Alice would avoid mirrors for the rest of her life. When asked if he had anything to say in mitigation, Mills had the nerve to ask for a lenient sentence:

"I hope you will have mercy on account of me being so short a time out of penal servitude."

It transpired that Mills had a habit of committing monstrous assaults on his nearest and dearest. Exhibit A, the first Mrs. Mills, similarly disfigured, was present in the court. Incensed by the offender's behaviour and lack of remorse, His Honour summed up as follows:

14. Women and hats and dog outside the General Peel Public House, Salford. The consumption of too much alcohol by inadequate husbands sometimes led to serious cases of wife-beating.

15. *Temperance societies took the fight against the evils of alcohol to the streets with limited effect.*

"I should think there is no brute in the whole of the county of Lancaster so brutal as you are, and so brutal as you have been, because it is not the first time you have been guilty of this same offence, and when you ask me to be merciful to you because you had only just come out of penal servitude, you surely forget altogether that I am aware of what the punishment was for and what you did that caused you to be sent into penal servitude. It is now just ten years since you were sentenced to ten years for throwing corrosive fluid over your then wife. You ill-treated her in exactly the same way. She lost her eye and is disfigured for life by your conduct. It is not brutal because it is far worse than that. No brute would behave in the way you have behaved… The least I can do to society and to the other poor women who might be placed in your power is to place it as far as I can beyond you ever to commit a similar offence. The sentence of the court is that you be kept in penal servitude for the rest of your life."

MURDEROUS ATTACKS ON WOMEN IN MANCHESTER

The normal pattern of domestic murder was for inadequate men to lose their tempers following disagreements or rejection. In 1879, 42-year-old William Cooper slit the throat of his paramour because she insisted on attending a dance despite his objections. The same year, following several rows, William Cassidy soaked his sleeping wife's bed in paraffin and set it alight. Both were hanged.

Returning home after a midday drinking session, 58-year-old Michael Kennedy flew into a rage when his wife of 36 years did not have his dinner on the table. When his better half later refused his sexual advances, saying that she did not kiss drunken men, Kennedy saw red. With no nosh nor nooky the frustrated inebriate went for his gun. He callously shot his wife in the head. Showing no remorse whatsoever as his wife lay dying in hospital, he told the police that he regretted not shooting her in the heart as *the job would have been done right.*

Michael Kennedy was hanged on December 30th 1872.

PUSHING A WIFE THROUGH A WINDOW

"George, don't put me through the window, for if you do I shall be killed."

George ignored the frantic plea and pushed his wife out of the opened bedroom window. Catherine Ellis fell 10' 4" to the hard, cold flagstones outside the home in William Street, Ardwick. A doctor was sent for but 51-year-old George Ellis, indifferent to the condition of his wife, simply returned to the pub.

16. Catherine Ellis died an agonising death in Ardwick one week after her husband pushed her through the window.

Catherine, the same age as her drunken partner, did not die on that Saturday in June 1871. She did, however, rupture her bladder, which in turn led to the peritonitis that eventually killed her.

The dazed, shocked woman was helped into her home and laid out on the sofa. That evening the insensitive brute she had chosen to marry returned from the pub at 11.30.p.m. in his now all too familiar state of intoxication. He demanded to sleep on the sofa. In front of two witnesses and, oblivious of his wife's agonising screams, Ellis sat on his wife's chest as if it were the sofa. Two neighbours caring for the distressed woman managed to move him into a chair.

One of the neighbours then asked Catherine whether she had taken her medicine. George Ellis roused from his drunken stupor and threw in his sixpenny worth. He insisted that she wanted no medicine; what she needed was a good hiding. Thankfully the wife-beater soon went to sleep.

Catherine herself went into the big sleep one week later.

Faced with a choice between manslaughter and murder, the jury opted for the more serious charge after twenty minutes deliberation. When asked if he had anything to say as to why sentence of death should not be passed, George Ellis thumped the edge of the dock and loudly proclaimed:

"I have this to say. I am innocent so help me God! I am innocent!"

Following his sentence Ellis seemed to console himself with a rather twisted logic:

"Well, it's a deal better to be hanged innocent than guilty."

THE MOSTON TRAGEDY 1888

"I die an innocent man. Lord have mercy on my soul. I am about to leave this earth for ever."

Adjusting the white cap, hangman Berry tugged at the lever. John Alfred Gell's drop to the floor below was halted at just five feet. For a full minute his body twitched and then all was still. He was cut down an hour later.

Gell was correct in one of his assertions; he did leave this earth for ever. He certainly did not die an innocent man. He died with the blood of kind-hearted Mary Miller on his hands.

From mid-January 1888, Gell had been staying in the same house as Mary and her daughter Isabella. The 32-year-old unemployed wheelwright could pay no rent and was tolerated at the Miller's house at number 6, St. Mary's road, Moston because Mary took pity on him. Like so many people who come to crash on the sofa for a few nights, Gell just would not leave. He mistook his landlady's kindness for affection and gradually became infatuated with the woman whose home he shared. Gell's affections were not reciprocated and Mary's daughter, positively detesting the cuckoo in the nest, persistently demanded that he decamp and inflict his presence on somebody else.

Some six weeks after installing himself with the Millers, Gell was revealing his feelings about Mary to a mutual friend:

"I love the woman, and am very fond of her. I will have her. If I don't no one else shall for I will finish her before anyone else shall have her."

The following evening both Mary Miller and John Gell visited the same friend. It was obvious that relations were very strained between the two. When the lodger attempted to kiss the landlady she spurned his advances:

"Go away from me, I hate you, I hate you: you must never enter my door any more Alfred Gell."

17. Jilted Gell would not accept that his landlady wanted nothing more to do with him.

Enraged at the public humiliation, Gell grabbed the woman he professed to love around the neck and dragged her out of the house insisting in his macho manner:

"Now you must go home. I will make you go home. Where you go I shall go."

The following morning Isabella rose at 6.a.m. to light the fire. She discovered a demented Gell pacing about the kitchen. He had not slept all night due to sickness. He knew she would offer neither sympathy nor tea, and Isabella simply said it served him right. Once again Isabella demanded to know when he would leave their lives for good. She refused to prepare him any breakfast and Gell stormed out of the house at 7.a.m. on March 1st 1888.

He returned at midday and informed a delighted Isabella that he had found a job and would soon be moving. Sitting on a stool with her back to the door Isabella smiled contentedly. Life would soon return to the old regime. Gell, meanwhile, was gingerly approaching the young woman from behind. Raising an axe he hacked it into the back of Isabella's skull.

Miraculously the youngster did not lose consciousness, but she was severely dazed. Mary rushed through to see what the commotion was about, whereupon Gell's infatuation turned to detestation.

When Isabella eventually managed to struggle to the back door and scream for help, a blood-soaked Gell finally left the Miller's home, scuttling off to go to ground in the maze of nearby houses.

A clearer account of the tragic events was revealed eight days later, on March 9th, when Gell gave himself up and made a statement to Police Sergeant Thompson. After being cautioned, Gell first enquired as to where Mary had been buried and then made the following confession:

"Ah, we should have lived happily together but for Bell. She was always calling me names. I went away to Newton Heath and returned and entered the house by the back door. Mrs. Miller saw me pick up the axe. I struck Bell in the front room. She screamed and Mrs. Miller who was washing, came to the door. When she saw Bell she ran back and was going out at the back door, when I struck her with the axe. She fell with her head on the closet step. She did not move only her eyes. I did it all in a few seconds."

This version however did not tally with the medical evidence. The surgeon summoned to the scene found Mary Miller slumped on a chair, alive but unconscious. Witnessing the amount of blood she had lost, the physician knew that she had little chance of survival and focused his attention on the wounded daughter whose life he managed to save.

18. The attempted murder of a sweetheart in Chorlton-on-Medlock.

The post-mortem examination of Mrs. Miller's body showed that the skull had been battered in. There were seven wounds on the head including two large fractures of the skull. They were caused by blows with the sharp edge of the axe delivered with great force.

At his trial Gell denied ever making a confession:

"I am not guilty, and I deny the statement made by Sergeant Thompson saying that I struck the mother with the axe."

The defence argued a weak case as best they could. A suspicious-looking man had been seen in the area about the time of the murder. It was halfheartedly advocated that this mystery stranger may have committed the act. When this was rejected Mr. Cottingham for the defence, clutching at yet another straw, argued that if Gell had wielded the axe, he must have been insane!

There could only be one verdict.

At a few minutes to eight on the day of execution, the hangman, Berry, entered Gell's cell with the Governor, prison surgeon, assistant-surgeon and under-sherrif. Gell's arms were pinioned. He was dressed in ordinary, not prison, clothes and had donned an overcoat, collar and tie for the occasion.

He walked towards the gallows firmly, showing few signs of distress.

Before his final protestations of innocence Gell had some words for the daughter he blamed for his predicament:

"Isabella Miller, I hope you have now had your revenge. Good bye. God bless you. "

ATTEMPTED MURDER OF A SWEETHEART

However much we may scoff at the sensationalist nature of its headlines, the exaggerated morbidity of its illustrations, the Victorian weekly, the *Illustrated Police News*, is as addictive today as it was over one hundred years ago. This story is from a May, 1888 edition:

William Walsh, a tall, strong-looking man, was charged before the Manchester city magistrates on Monday, last week, with attempting to murder a girl named Winifred Higgins, sixteen, with whom he had been keeping company, by throwing her into the Medlock.

It appeared that about half-past three o'clock on

19. Amelia Moss appears to have been fixated on the idea of marriage. She received six months hard labour for stealing two rings in 1875 and three months for bigamy in 1900.

Monday morning, Police Constable Cooper, whilst on duty in London-road, heard screams proceeding from the direction of Boardman-street. He at once ran to ascertain the cause, and on looking over some railings dividing Boardman-street from the River Medlock, he saw a girl sitting in the water, which at that place is about eighteen inches deep. Procuring a ladder the constable got the girl out, and at once conveyed her to the Royal Infirmary.

She informed him that her name was Winifred Higgins and added that on Saturday night she met her sweetheart, William Walsh, in Higher Ormond street and went with him to a public-house where he had some drink. She, however, did not have any. Afterwards Walsh took her to some place where she did not know and acted improperly towards her. The two then walked together as far as Boardman-street, and when they reached the railings already referred to they had a few words. Higgins said she was frightened to go home, and Walsh replied with an oath that she could go home at any time. After some further words he caught hold of her by the waist, and, lifting her over the railings, which are six feet high, dropped her into the river, a distance of thirty or thirty-five feet.

In consequence of the girl's statement, Acting-sergeant Ruby at once went to Walsh's residence and arrested him in bed. He said to the officer it had been a 'quick job.' When charged at the station with attempted murder prisoner said he was not guilty.

The case was transferred to the Liverpool Assizes.

A CAGED BIRD

One must feel some sympathy for John James Bird. In 1861 he married for the second time in Stockport at the age of 42. It was without a doubt the biggest mistake of his life. On three separate occasions his new wife, Bridget Malkin, sold off all the family possessions: furniture, clothes, kitchen utensils, anything she could get her hands on, was pawned and squandered on drink. Twice John forgave her, but on the third occasion Bridget did not wait for forgiveness; she fled to America. Not only had she pawned the contents of their home, but she had also abandoned her three children from a previous marriage, whom she regularly threatened when in her cups. For their own safety John had earlier sent them to live with a relation in Macclesfield. With his wife now 3,000 miles away the brow-beaten husband regained his good humour and began associating with other women.

When Bridget's brother told him that she had died in New Hampshire, John went for a celebratory pint and popped the question to the new love in his life, Mary Hart. The couple married in 1869. Unfortunately, like the bad penny she was, Bridget turned up in Manchester shortly afterwards. Reports of her death had been greatly exaggerated.

John agreed to make a regular weekly payment for her maintenance in the workhouse but when he could no longer afford the contributions, Bridget carried out her threat and blew the whistle, denouncing him as a bigamist.

Bird was caged for six months.

ONCE A THIEF...

Court reporting has changed over the years with the advent of political correctness. In the nineteenth century court reporters had no reservations when describing the accused. Most of the following pen portraits were written by journalists for the *Manchester City News*, they describe people one would not like to brush up against in a dark alley. The following list is fairly representative:

An old, haggard looking woman
A female of pallid appearance
A portly middle-aged man
A termagant looking member of the "gentler" sex
A grey-haired ill-looking man
A ruffianly fellow
A dirty faced boy
A good-looking robust young woman
A powerfully built young fellow of ferocious appearance
A gaudily-apparelled female
A vicious-looking vixen
An individual whose physiognomy and accent unmistakenly indicated his Israelitish origin
A scampish looking character
An unbonnetted female, whose 'personelle' was certainly the reverse of attraction
A dark cadaverous-looking individual
A fiery-faced female aged forty
A wretched-looking imbecile
A middle-aged person of deprived mien
A ragged, greasy, voluble tramp
A ragged little street arab

The English used in some of the charges would today be considered a little O.T.T. In 1882, Mary Holland, a laundress was sent down for nine months' hard labour, for being:

An incorrigible rogue, for that she, the said Margaret Holland, then being a common prostitute, did on the 20th March 1882 unlawfully wander in the public streets, and behave in a riotous and indecent manner after having been previously convicted of being a rogue and vagabond.

Newspapers reported from the courts with some relish often with eye-catching headlines such as **BITING A MAN'S EAR OFF** (*Manchester City News,* March 15th, 1875). Details of the story are as follows.

In the spring of 1875 Henry Wheeler from Dyers-lane was downing a bevvy or two with John Hughes at a beer house in Fleat street, Deansgate. Before the days of United and City, locals would use any excuse to set about each other. Henry and John soon started quarrelling about a broken beer jug. Both men stepped outside but no sooner were they in the fresh air than Henry assaulted John in what the newspapers conservatively described as *pretty revolting circumstances.*

20. *Paddy the Devil (Patrick Cox, 39 in 1893). A notorious counterfeiter who apparently was not too keen on having his own likeness duplicated.*

21. There was always a ready market for stolen and second-hand boots and hats.

Henry Wheeler savaged John Hughes, making several attempts to bite Hughes about the face. He eventually got the poor fellow's ear between his teeth and bit it clean off. Margaret Swindell, a witness, said that she heard Wheeler say that he would chew Hughes to pieces. She picked the ear off the floor, but without the technology that over a century later would come to John Wayne Bobbit's rescue, poor John Hughes had to bear the scars for the rest of his life.

Henry Wheeler was committed for trial.

CRIME IN THE 1860s

Of approximately 13,000 arrests in the Manchester area in 1866, almost half were on drink related charges. Indeed grog was the common thread running through crime statistics throughout the period, from minor theft to murder and manslaughter. With over 2,000 beerhouses in Manchester, one for every 130 inhabitants, the local was just that; its temptations too great.

One in three of those apprehended were women, who showed the wild side of their natures *by tearing each other's clothes, rolling each other in the dirt and tearing the hair from each other's heads.* This small proportion of criminals was responsible for a substantial number of recorded offences, with approximately one in twelve arrests being for prostitution.

In 1867-68 Manchester police estimated the number of brothels at 325, housing some 809 prostitutes. Other estimates seem to be on the conservative side (an early case of manipulating the figures?). Three years later, with a population of 173,000 in Manchester, 83,000 in Salford, there were an estimated 214 low lodging houses; 70 houses keeping stolen goods; 710 reputed thieves and 322 persons known *occasionally to steal.*

The occupations of those arrested were, in order of frequency: labourers; factory workers and weavers; prostitutes; mechanics and metal workers; miscellaneous trades; charwomen and needle women; housekeepers; carters and coachmen; hawkers; joiners.

The following chart, chosen entirely at random, shows a typical day's proceedings :

CASES AT THE SALFORD HUNDREDS MARCH 2, 1867

NAME	AGE	PROFESSION	OFFENCE	SENTENCE
Thomas Tweedale	30	factory operator	stealing shawl	7yrs.
Ashton Wroe	32	labourer	embezzling £1.3s.6d.	3mths
Ann Johnson	44	charwoman	stealing from clothes line	2mths
William Stannard	22	sweep	stealing half-crown (13p)	7yrs.
Ann Donavan	26	hawker	stealing 2 blankets, 1 sheet	4mths
John Fletcher	29	bricklayer	stealing 57 yards of wincey	7yrs.
Henry Bleckly	20	dyer	stealing 8 hens and 1 cock	3mths
Mary Power	15	servant	stealing clothes	18mths
Elizabeth Fildes	22	servant	stealing 7lbs. bread	4 mths
Ellen Meadowcroft	28	servant	stealing clothes	1 mth
William Roberts	42	labourer	stealing clothes	1 mth
David Tomlinson	17	hosiery trimmer	stealing a pair of boots	18mths
Michael Green	13	factory operative	stealing waistcoat and 2 keys	1mth*
Margaret Walker	37	hawker	stealing one pair of stockings	2yrs

Michael's month inside was followed by five years in an industrial school.
The apparent inconsistencies of sentencing can be explained by the offender's previous record. Those sentenced to 7 years will inevitably have had a long string of convictions, which they had failed to conceal.

8,000 of those apprehended could read and write after a fashion, they being noted as *imperfects*, a term reserved for the semi-literate. 4,000, about one in three, couldn't read at all, while 500 – one in 25 – were of *superior education*, that is they could read and write well. In terms of ethnicity, over 9,000 of those arrested were English, while some 3,500 were of Irish origin – fairly recent arrivals who'd experienced difficulties settling in.

With crime statistics high in comparison with other cities, Manchester was a dangerous place to live.

Following the public hanging of three Fenians, relations between Catholics and Protestants were tense. In June, 1869, 9-year-old Ellen Higgins was making her way along Little Peter street with several other girls her own age. Their path was blocked by four boys a little older than themselves. They were immediately challenged as to their religion. When the girls declined to take off their green ribbons they were so viciously attacked that Ellen suffered brain damage and other internal injuries from which she later died.

In 1865 an outbreak of what was then termed garrotting, led to a public demand for stiffer sentencing. Mancunians could not walk the streets for fear of being set upon by small gangs. They would approach the victim from behind and with the forearm cut off the air-supply by applying pressure to the Adam's apple. Panic-stricken citizens avoided walking the streets at night after reading reports of attacks involving *the crushing of the throat, leaving the victim writhing in agony, with tongue protruding and eyes staring from their sockets, unable to give the alarm or attempt a pursuit..*

Mr. Justice Lush sent 23 garrotters to gaol, ordering each to make the acquaintance of the *cat* on three separate occasions at the start of their sentence. This part of the punishment had often been left to the week before release so offenders had something to look forward to throughout their custodial sentence.

The bravado of youth was evident in the early stages of judicial flagellation, when the pinioned young man would often unwisely bait the flogger with taunts:

"Lay it on."
"My mother could do better than that."
"You wouldn't do for a schoolmaster."

Gradually they fell silent before the inevitable cries for mercy.

THE RING-DROPPING SCAM

Cockney Jim was the master of the ring-dropping scam, a highly successful trick played on the public of Manchester in the 1860-70s.

22. Pickpockets would mingle amongst buyers and sellers in the crowded markets.

23. *The pawnbrokers, destination of many stolen goods.*

Jim would firstly buy a set of cheap gold rings for a few shillings each, and, with the help of a forged mark, were made to appear to be worth considerably more than their original purchase price. For the con, Jim needed an assistant or 'sharp'. Both men would go to one of the more prosperous areas of the city to seek out a likely victim.

With the prey selected the 'sharp' walks past him and, bending down, pretends to pick something up from off the pavement. This 'find' is one of the phoney gold rings which he examines, a self satisfied broad smile spreading across his face. Out of curiosity the victim is anxious to see what has just been found. If he is not of the curious nature the 'sharp' approaches and informs him of his good luck.

Just by chance Jim, another bypasser who has, of course, never met the 'sharp' before, approaches. He is invited to join the pair and questioned as to his evaluation of the find. Adopting an informed attitude, Jim values the ring at between £10 and £20 and implores the finder to sell it to him for that price if he will go to the house with him to collect the cash. Arguing that he is already late for work and will lose his post if not on time the 'sharp' refuses the offer. Meanwhile the victim's brain is going into overdrive. He listens as the 'sharp' states that he will take £2 for the ring and Jim curse, saying he would surely take it but does not have the money in his possession. Feeling in his pocket the victim produces two sovereigns and begs the 'finder' to sell to him. Jim storms off in a huff. The 'sharp' pockets the £2 and the victim smiles all the way to work.

It's a different story that afternoon, however, as Jim and the 'sharp' quaff ale in a beerhouse and the victim stops for an evaluation at the jewellers.

BEFORE THE BEAK

So what happened when offenders were brought to justice in the 1860s?

There was certainly little consistency in sentencing and when tried before a jury -all male – the verdicts were singly unpredictable. In 1868 an article, *In the Jury Box,* appeared in the *Manchester City News*. It held the whole judicial system up to mild ridicule. After describing the room used for the trial of prisoners at New Bailey Salford, as *a dingy, uncongenial place smelling of damp and policemen* the reporter turned his attention to the make-up of the court's juries:

Juries are composed of queer materials sometimes; men of all qualifications and some with

24. Elizabeth Turner (49) alias Mary Black, Margaret Graham, Margaret Rogers, Margaret Farmer, Margaret Rylauch and Theresa Mack. She took pride in her appearance but did not believe in paying for her clothes. She was convicted on numerous occasions from 1886 of stealing hats, frocks, jackets, shoes, dresses, shawls and boots.

none. Addle-headed crotchety fellows, who can see no further than their nose end, are jostled together with sharp-eyed, quick-witted intelligent men.

One jury found a man not guilty and then expressed hope he would not do it again!

Another enlightened group reported back to the judge:

If the prisoner at the bar committed the crime he was guilty, but if he didn't then he was not.

A third pronounced a prisoner: *Guilty and served him right for being caught.*

A fourth more liberal group found a prisoner *Guilty but recommended to mercy on account of his long imprisonment.*

Upon discharge, jurors had to pay one shilling to ensure that they would not be called for the unremunerated job for the next two years. Failure to present for jury service resulted in a fine of £5. Jurors dreaded longer cases for it could mean being locked away overnight and fed only bread and cheese!

Women inevitably suffered at the hands of all-male juries. In rape cases the onus was on them to prove that they had physically fought their attacker and not consented in any way. With cases of wife-beating and manslaughter the jury and judge often sympathised with a fellow male who pleaded that he had been taunted, nagged and provoked by the woman he assaulted.

A case in Ancoats, 1874, seems typical of the period and helps to illustrate the thinking of some men of the time. On March 21 of that year, Michael Kilbride was submitted for trial on a charge of manslaughter. His actions had resulted in the death of his sister-in-law in a pub brawl one month previously. He openly admitted to having started the fight by giving his opponent '*a hefty blow on the head*', which knocked her down. His victim, Ellen, immediately retaliated by throwing a jug at her attacker. It missed and Kilbride struck another heavy blow, this time with a clenched fist. He continued the assault with a series of bone-crushing kicks to the body, then dragged the half-conscious woman to the stairway and pushed her down. Still not finished, he raced down the stairs, wrenched his victim to her feet and battered her head against the door as he dragged her out.

Kilbride was found guilty of manslaughter, with a recommendation for mercy on account of provocation. Poor Ellen had dared to throw a jug at her assailant!

The offender was sent down for twelve months

WHERE THERE'S POOR PEOPLE THERE'S THIEVES

Women not averse to breaking the law, but reluctant to turn to prostitution, had a whole variety of scams to fall back on in order to earn a dishonest crust. Most were petty opportunist thieves, forever on the lookout for a quick hit. The odd month or two spent in prison was just a hazard of the profession.

In 1874 Irish Kate was nearing the end of her criminal – and any other – career. She was described in the *Manchester Evening News* as '*a withered dried-up specimen with a little puckered-up face… sucking the stem of her pipe with great gusto. She had the dirtiest pipe, the rankest weed and the most garrulous tongue .*'

Her favourite story related to the theft of a huge piece of cheese which took her fancy. When she sensed that the grocer was not looking, Kate lifted the giant wedge, and holding it tight to her chest

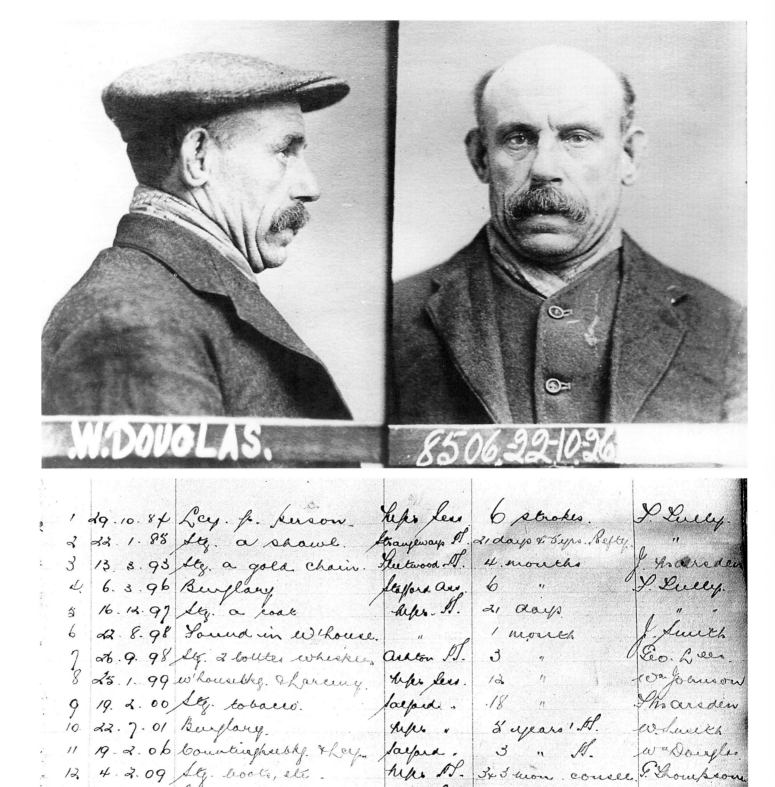

1	29.10.84	Lcy. fr. Person	Seps Sess	6 strokes	P. Gully
2	22.1.85	Stg. a shawl	Strangeways PS	21 days & 5 yrs. Refy.	"
3	13.3.93	Stg. a gold chain	Fleetwood PS.	4 months	J. Marsden
4	6.3.96	Burglary	Stafford Ass	6 "	P. Gully
5	16.12.97	Stg. a coat	Seps. PS.	21 days	"
6	22.8.98	Found in W'house	"	1 month	J. Smith
7	26.9.98	Stg. 2 bottles whiskey	Ashton PS.	3 "	Geo. Lee
8	25.1.99	W'housebkg & Larceny	Seps Sess	12 "	Wm Johnson
9	19.2.00	Stg. tobacco	Salford	18 "	S. Marsden
10	22.7.01	Burglary	Seps	5 years' H.	W. Smith
11	19.2.06	Countinghsebkg & Lcy	Salford	3 " H.	Wm Douglas
12	4.2.09	Stg. boots, etc	Seps PS.	3x3 mon. consec	P. Thompson
13	21.3.10	Shopbkg & Lcy (5 cases)	Seps Sess	12.12.12 mon. consec	W Douglas
14	20.3.11	Attempted Burglary	"	18 months	"
15	25.5.11	Countinghsebkg & Lcy	"	3 years' H.	"
16	20.12.23	Shopbreaking	Ashton Boro.	Handed over to asylum authorities	"
17	21.10.25	W'housebkg & Larceny	Preston QS.	1 month	
18	1.4.26	Stg. iron bar & piece lead	Bolton Co.	1 "	J.C.O.R.E. Geo. Mortimer
19	—	Found on our premises	—	Found insane	W. Douglas
20	18.10.26	Shopbkg & Larceny	Knutsford Sess	Detained H.M. Pleasure	

25. The 6 strokes William Douglas received in 1884 appear to have been no deterrent. His long career as a burglar ended when he was found to be insane and detained at His Majesty's pleasure.

made off down the main street. Hearing the dreaded cries of 'Stop! Thief!' several yards behind her, Kate realised she would have to discard her intended supper and threw the cheese to one side of the road. When challenged by a policeman the street-wise Irishwoman denied all knowledge of the stolen food. When the cheese was recovered, however, there was an unfamiliar indented pattern which had not been on it at the grocer's shop. The indentations were a perfect match of the buttons on Kate's dress, made as she had clutched her booty so tightly. Irish Kate felt herself leniently treated telling the reporter:

"I got off wid two months."

A LIFE OF CRIME

Reviewing the mug shots and records of Victorian criminals, it is remarkable how long some people continued to offend, often to well past our retirement age. Judging by their faces, a lot of them aged long before their time, but some continued well into their seventies: crime was their only way of life, with many spending the bulk of their lives behind bars.

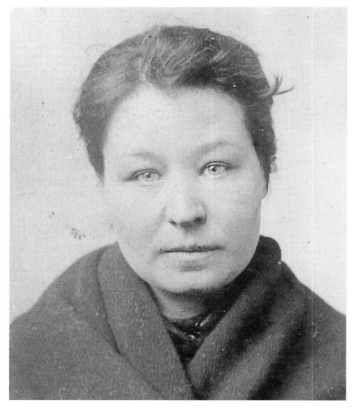

26. A woman with an identity problem. Mary Davies (if that was her real name) was prosecuted for petty theft under the names of Anne Cawley (1886), Hannah M Dixon (1886), Annie Lloyd (1886), Mary A Williams (1886), Mary Richards (1887), Mary Kelly (1889), Mary Richardson (1890) and Mary Farrell (1890).

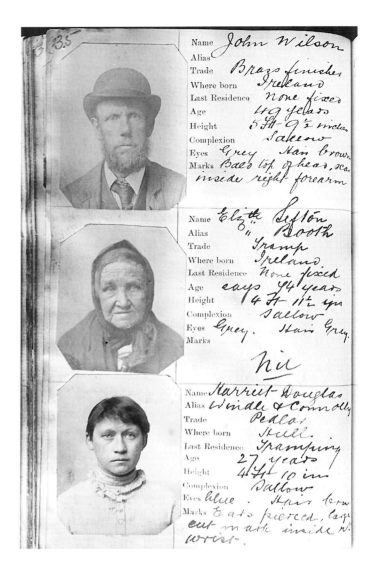

27. With the onset of old-age professional thieves had to change their modus operandi. Elizabeth Sefton, who said she was 74, turned to stealing from clothes lines. So much about the past can be learnt from so few words. Harriet Douglas, just 4' 10" tall, a 27-year-old peddler, hawked her goods from town to town. The large scar on the inside of her wrist may have been the result of attempted suicide. One cannot help but wonder what became of characters like Harriet Douglas, alias Windle, alias Connolly. Her choices in life were limited. Did she follow the path of Elizabeth Sefton?

No matter how spartan prison conditions, or how heavy the fines, some women simply persevered with their criminal ways until they were no longer physically capable. Margaret Gerrety and May Clynes seemed to be in a race to see who could score the first century of drunk and disorderly convictions. Appearing in court on the same day, Margaret was convicted for the 89th time and May (known as Toffee Polly) for the 84th. Both were fined 10s. 6d. or the option of one month in prison.

Emma Howarth appeared before the courts in 1864 for the 106th time for being drunk and disorderly. It appears the drink had gone to her head, for she was described as 'an unbonneted

28. One-eyed Annie Kelly, Queen of the habitual offenders with over 69 prosecutions for theft, drunkenness, prostitution and indecent exposure.

female whose personelle was certainly the reverse of attractive'. When fined five shillings, or six days in default, Emma honestly replied that she did not even have five farthings.

Mary Ann Williamson notched up her ton of convictions in the 1880s. She was found 'guilty' on more than 104 occasions, in Manchester and Salford, on charges of being a disorderly prostitute, a thief and a drunkard.

Ann Welsh, 62, was accused of stealing 2 petticoats, 2 dresses, 2 sheets, 2 skirts, 2 pairs of stockings and one tablecloth. Ann, however, could turn her hand to anything: her record included 20 convictions for assault, drunkenness and umpteen other felonies.

At 63, Ann Davies was convicted, 11th August 1885, for having 'feloniously, wilfully and of her malice afterthought, killed and murdered one Paul Davies.' Found to be temporarily insane, she was ordered to be kept in custody until Her Majesty's pleasure be known.

The queen of recidivists must surely have been one-eyed Annie Kelly. In court in 1923, it was observed the 58-year-old, **aka** Rattigan, Rattican, Burns and Jones, had so many convictions no charge book was big enough to record them. Her offences, including the theft of money, stockings, purses etc; indecent exposure, drunkenness and prostitution, were block-booked under Previous Convictions x 69.

Alice Sinclair was another old sot, who couldn't leave the bottle alone. The hawker, who also answered to the name of Nellie Brookes and Maggi Clarke, appeared at Strangeways police court in 1928 for being found drunk. It was her 90th offence.

Described as 'an elderly dame' Ellen Grace, **aka** McCoy, Murphy and Burke, was caught red-handed with one hand in another lady's pocket. Ellen thanked the magistrate when he gave her three months – a fairly light sentence given her list of previous convictions.

Like so many women, before and after her, Matilda Vear's weakness was clothing she couldn't afford. The laundress, however, had her own solution to the problem. She started stealing in 1896 and was repeatedly charged for taking away without paying, her haul included a fur boa; a sealskin jacket; five pieces of cloth; skirts; a dress;

29. Leon Lampford and coat. Fraudsters and con-men have long taken a pride in their appearance. Convicted in Manchester in July 1878 for selling sea passages to clerks with the promise of a job in the Cape. Both job and passage existed only in Leon's devious mind.

30. A photo from the early days of police intelligence gathering. Officers in Manchester were warned to look out for 'Jimmy the Greek', a 'swell' London and continental hotel thief and pickpocket.

one straw hat and one pair of boots. For these offences, coupled with two convictions for drunkenness, Matilda served a total of 29 months. Released in 1903 at the age of 46, she was almost immediately re-arrested for stealing two skirts.

THE CRIMINAL CAREER OF JOHN WILSON BORN 1841

During the forty year period 1857-96 John Wilson spent more than 32 years in prison. The total value of the goods he stole was less than £3. This was not the end of his criminal career, however. He kept on thieving – and getting caught – into the early years of the twentieth century.

DATE	GOODS STOLEN	SENTENCE
1857	sweets	6 days (whipped)
1859	sweets	3 months
1861	tea	6 months
1861	handkerchief	6 months
1862	dress piece	3 months
1864	money	4 years
1867	money	10 years
1878	money	14 years
1889	attempted larceny	18 months
1892	frequenting	3 months
1893	attempt to steal	12 months
1894	purse	12 months
1896	frequenting	3 months

In the early years of the twentieth century, one known pickpocket – well past his cell-by date! – was spotted by Detective-Inspector Ashton expertly dipping through the city. The experienced hand held an overcoat over one arm to conceal his movements, but was observed fingering the folds of a lady's dress. When he moved into Victoria Street, he was seen to repeat the offence four times. Patrick McHugh, who'd apparently lost his touch, was subsequently convicted of loitering with intent and sentenced to three months. When his record was read out in court, it was revealed that he had already served sentences of four, ten and fourteen years' penal servitude and had long been numbered among the quaintly termed *incorrigibles* .

Despite their lengthy records, some suspects never put their hands up. Our final story concerning offenders old enough to know better is taken directly from a local newspaper:

AN INDIGNANT PRISONER

John Frederick Harrison, an elderly man who is known at the City Police Court for his glibness, was again before the magistrates today, charged with the usual offence of pocket picking. Detective-Inspector Ashton and Detective Davison, who arrested him in the neighbourhood of St Ann's Square, gave evidence of the prisoner's efforts, and Harrison was very indignant. "This is the fourth time," he said, "that I have been here for this sort of thing. I have never dreamed of picking a lady's pocket, and the story of the detective has been deliberately concocted." Three months' imprisonment was the sentence.

JUVENILE CRIME

In the 1860's, attendance at such schools as there were, was patchy. For many children, education took place on the streets. They quickly learnt that no money meant no food and some became adept at petty theft and pilfering, showing

(Insp. Henderson)

Manchester Police

Insp. Gill

James Cooke. —

A Dealer in the Market Place, Wigan — and a Receiver of Stolen goods — 40. 5 ft 5. brown eyes. dark brown hair — fresh complexion — brown whiskers — stout made. Scar over side of left eye —

Apprehend on 26ᵗʰ October 1871 in the Act of stealing a quantity of fancy goods from Bradford's Warehouse 44 Shudehill in conjunction with one of the Servants there named Daniel Brown

Charles Collingwood.

A Hotel thief — called himself a ship's steward — 26 or 28 — 5 ft. 10 — sallow complexion — grey eyes — dark brown hair and dark moustache — Stout built —

Sentenced to 7 Years Penal Servitude — Jan. 1871. for a robbery at "The Clarence" —

Got 18 mos previously in Edin Shff Court — under the name of John Black — (9 Nov. 1868) Detective J. Walker of Edin proved that conviction —

Thomas Welsh —

A thief repeatedly convicted — 25 — 5 ft 7 — fresh complexion — black hair — black eyes — long nose — shaved whiskers — imperfectly educated — belongs to L'pool — B.C. on right side — Anchor, V. R. & colours, crown, cross & swords on fore arm — Crucifix, stars, colours, cross swords &.g tatooed on right fore arm — bracelets on wrists — Released from Carlisle Gaol on 26 Dec. 1871.

31. Police forces throughout the country began compiling their own mug shot albums. Some were portraits taken from the offender's home, others taken under police instruction at a local studio.

guile and cunning way beyond their years. Some limited their aims to stealing the packed breakfasts left by carters and labourers on their wagons. Others were more ambitious.

The more cunning, begged from door to door in the hope that their age and dishevelled appearance would prompt acts of charity. In 1864, 12-year-old Ellen Murphy called at the house of the kindly Mrs. Kershaw. Ellen rubbed her stomach and raised her eyes to the sky, she was famished she said, and would do anything for a little money to buy food. Mrs. Kershaw asked the starving waif to undertake a small washing job but Ellen was not there to help the good lady, she was there to help herself and tucked a flannel shirt below her cape. She was spotted by the eagle-eyed housekeeper and stopped in her tracks, doubtless with the immortal line, "I can see you sneaking out."

Ellen's attempt to make off early and avoid embarrassment had been thwarted. She later admitted to two similar offences, with one shirt being sold and the other pledged.

Juveniles preyed, solo or in small gangs, on other children. Anyone a year or two younger, an inch or two shorter, could be set upon in the streets and relieved of parcels, money or food, anything of resale value. Some unfortunate children were even

33. The real John Smith, a young and spectacularly unsuccessful housebreaker. He wasted nearly all his youth in reformatories and prison. When the photo was taken in 1883 he was about to start a five stretch for shop-breaking.

stripped of all their clothes and forced to scurry home naked.

The common destination of stolen clothes was the pawnbroker or second hand markets, just as stolen goods today often end up in boot sales. Child-stripping was not solely the domain of young offenders, though, it often became the last resort of hardened female recidivists, who had neither the strength nor speed to commit other crimes.

Older children wandered the streets in gangs looking for easy prey or simply just out to make mischief. A favourite ruse was to accost female churchgoers on their way home, all the while shouting lewd and sexist insults. The bolder boys attempted to snatch shawls and bonnets.

Children brought up by hardened criminals rarely escaped the apprenticeship of petty theft, industrial school, drunkenness, short prison sojourns, parenthood, prison and so on. Bad habits were picked up at a very early age and the success rates of missions in changing behaviour were small. The indefatigable missionary Alsop was almost in despair as he described the wasted lives of children in Deansgate in the 1870's:

32. Henry Wilson alias (believe it or not) John Smith. Despite his youthful appearance he had done the circuit of Britain's gaols, being convicted in Bristol, Bootle, Liverpool, Glasgow and Manchester. When arrested he was identified by no fewer than 127 children he had robbed on the streets.

A word about the children. Around us there are about a thousand children in a very small space. They are reared – or I should say dragged – up in wickedness. As soon as a child – poor thing! – begins to speak it is taught to swear, for the amusement of these barbarians; and young children of three, four and five years of age are adepts in swearing. From six to twelve years of age they can drink; and – something fearful! – from twelve to sixteen their knowledge and education of low life, houses of sin, &c. is complete.

Before young men and boys were flogged they were examined by the police sergeant. This was a rather perfunctory process, partly with psychological cruelty in mind. The dreaded anticipation of the thrashing was almost as painful as the act itself. Slowly and methodically the offender would be securely strapped to the horse. When the wrists and ankles were similarly restricted a body belt was fitted to the back. Only when firmly secure did the beating begin and cries and screams similar to those below, followed every sickening swish:

After the first: *"Oh! Oh!! Oh!!!"*
second: *"Murder!"*
third: *"You're killing me!"*
fourth: *"Oh! Mother."*
fifth: *"I'll never do it again."*
sixth: *"Do stop him!"*

Young males were rarely beaten more than once, this form of punishment being deemed usually appropriate for a **first** offence. Below is a random sample of boys and young men thrashed towards the end of the last century.

SCUTTLING

Scuttling, a form of gang warfare, was a recurring problem for Lancashire police forces throughout the latter part of the nineteenth century. Early reports speak of groups of males, aged ten years to (at least physical) maturity, deliberately setting about each other with clogs, belts, buckles and home-made weapons. Robbery was not the motivation.

34. Uriah Sharples received 6 strokes for shoplifting as a 15-year-old. He was back in court again the following year.

By the 1890s girls had joined the gangs and mixed groups slashed at each other with razors and knives. On one occasion the Ordsall Lane Gang and the Hope Street Gang ran into each other in a beer house near Oldfield Street. A match on neutral ground in Hampson Street was duly arranged. Shortly after kick-off, the two sides set about each other with belts, sticks and knives. Four lads were seriously injured with stab wounds and four arrests resulted in convictions of between four and eight months.

A police constable told the court about the behaviour of scuttlers in battle. When they needed help, males would give a short shrill whistle and females a special sort of high-pitched scream. Few deaths resulted from scuttling.

DATE	NAME	AGE	CRIME	PUNISHMENT
1880	James Wright	15	stealing pair of boots	11 strokes of the birch
1882	Arthur Seddon	7 or 8	stealing neckerchief	4 strokes
1886	Charles Jones	8	stealing socks	8 strokes
1890	James Waugh	16	stealing 4 pigeons	6 strokes
1892	Walter Ball	13	stealing cakes	12 strokes
1893	John Derbyshire*	10	stealing cloth	4 strokes
1896	Peter Costello	18	stealing pair of boots	12 strokes

*Who knows the effect the beating had on poor John Derbyshire. Nine years later he was sentenced to 6 months for the crime of *'feloniously, wickedly and against the order of nature knowing a cow'*!

IN THE CORONER'S COURT

For the very young the family home was probably the most dangerous place to be. In the 1860's one in four children did not survive their first year.

CASES IN THE CORONER'S COURT
MARCH – APRIL 1871

M/F	AGE	CAUSE OF DEATH
01 F	24	fell down a cellar
02 F	33	complications following a broken leg
03 F	41	suicide by drowning
04 F	23	burned to death
05 F	2	accident in kitchen
06 M	2d	asphyxia
07 F	10w	discovered frothing at the mouth
08 M	6	burned to death
09 M	2	inflammation of lungs
10 M	44	strong winds brought down shop faceboard
11 M	52	hanged himself in police cell
12 F	60	burned to death
13 M	?	slipped off platform in front of train
14 F	16	killed by exploding powder flask
15 M	30	road accident – horse and cart
16 F	13m	found dead in bed
17 M	3	drowned in canal
18 F	3	burned to death
19 F	6	overdose of Jilap (Jalap?)
20 M	18m	convulsions
21 F	3m	found dead in bed
22 M	6w	found dead in bed
23 F	14m	found dead with clothes over face
24 M	20m	kitchen accident
25 F	3	burnt by boiling water
26 M	44	concussion of the brain
27 F	2m	found dead in bed
28 F	5w	found dead in bed
29 F	4m	found dead in bed
30 M	6w	found dead in bed
31 F	18	fell down trap door
32 M	35	heart attack
33 F	16m	passed away as mother was washing her
34 M	3	burned in accident
35 M	40	building accident
36 F	5m	sat upon in cradle by drunken father

M/F male/female d = days w = weeks m = months

THE VICTORIAN WAY OF DEATH

Over half the above cases involved children below the age of five years. Although the dangers of families sleeping in the same bed were known, money was so scarce that even primitive cribs, which may have saved lives, were too expensive. Families who did own cots were sometimes forced to chop them up for firewood during bitingly cold Manchester winters. Unguarded fires accounted for several deaths of unsupervised children, or drunken adults. The problem was worsened by the clothing of the day, whose highly inflammable natural fibres rapidly became engulfed in flames.

How many child deaths were deliberate and how many accidental, is open to conjecture. Death amongst children under five was so commonplace that few people cared whether a parent had intentionally asphyxiated their sleeping child or not. It can be no coincidence that the death rate of infants born out of wedlock was more than double that of those born to married parents.

Let's look in more detail at the infant deaths above. No names were listed in the reports from the Coroner's Court so we need to refer to the children by number.

No. 5, a 2-year-old girl, lived with her mother in a court off Ludgate Hill. The parent worked as a hawker and was away from home all day. She left her baby in the charge of an elderly widow. Whilst her keeper's back was turned the little girl pulled a cup of steaming tea over herself and was badly scolded 'all down her chest.' She was taken to a druggist, where some 'stuff' was put on. The mother could not afford to call in a doctor and the child was not taken to the infirmary. A painful lingering death followed. At the Coroner's Court the mother, described as 'a strong broad-chested and not ill-looking woman' answered questions about the deaths of her other children – in total 4 out of 8 had perished in infancy:

CORONER: 'Have you lost any children before by accident?'

MOTHER: 'No, certainly not; they all died natural, and I have buried three before.'

The bereaved parent gave the impression that she regarded the arrival of babies in much the same spirit as we would regard buses on Oxford Road – it's neither here nor there to miss one.

Following her other losses, however, the mother

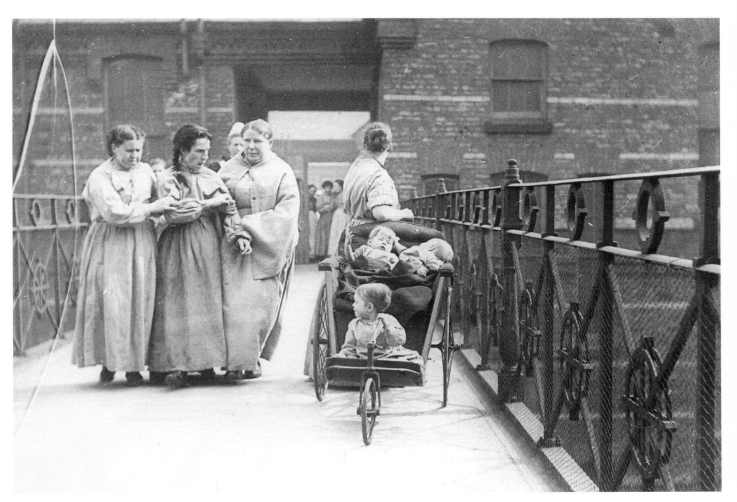

35. Children at the Crumpsall Workhouse Infirmary mixed with paupers who were both mentally and physically ill (c.1897).

had sensibly insured the newly deceased and fifty shillings were paid upon her daughter's death.

No.6, a two-day-old boy, died from suffocation. The mother, a factory-operative from Bury and none too bright, did not realise she was pregnant, thinking instead that she was suffering from a tumour. The baby was found to be a healthy child, but, despite the suspicious circumstances, no further action was taken.

No. 8, a boy who, at six, had survived the dangerous years, died because of his fascination with fire. His clothes caught fire in the bedroom.

The report on No.9 is taken directly from the *Manchester City News*:

A boy, aged two years, the illegitimate son of a single woman, a laundress. A fortnight ago the child had fallen over the hearthrug on to the fender, receiving a cut, which bled. No doctor was consulted, and some other ailment being meantime added, the child grew much worse. Being at length alarmed, a doctor was seen, who could only tell the mother to take it home, as it was then dying. The medical witness stated the cause of death to be inflammation of the lungs, and that life might have been saved by prompt medical aid. The deceased child was in a club.

The following account for No. 16 is typical of *'found dead in bed'* cases:

A female infant, aged thirteen months, without mother. The child was sleeping with its aunt, and two other children – four in the same bed. It had not been well and teething was complained of. It was found dead next morning at seven.

No 19 must have led the most miserable six years of life imaginable on this planet. The family lived, appropriately, in Dark Lane, Ardwick. The deceased's mother was described as being 'half-imbecile' and unable to give sensible or satisfactory answers; her father appeared at the Coroner's Court following a long session in the local. The mother was no better nurse than she was communicator. When she found her daughter ailing she administered an extremely large dose of 'Jilap' (Jalap?), possibly a popular remedy for stomach pains. The medical examination showed extensive internal disease and inflammation.

No. 24, a boisterous baby boy aged 20 months, was tied into a rocking chair in the kitchen. With the baby not having a father, his mother had to go out to work and the baby was left in a shared house. Whilst his carer was out of the kitchen, the baby

36. Eagle Street, Smithfield Market 1907. Though not the problem we have today, many children were injured and killed in traffic accidents.

37. The prisoner could face no more bird. After weeks of alcohol abuse, he hanged himself on his first day of sobriety.

rocked himself so hard that he fell, bringing down a large saucepan of boiling water and potatoes over himself. He succumbed to his injuries at the infirmary.

No. 36, the death of this five-month-old girl should surely have resulted in some form of criminal charge. Her father had been drinking heavily throughout Sunday lunchtime. In the early evening he returned and started arguing and beating his wife, who fled the family home. When she calculated that he would have sobered up, the apprehensive woman returned to her baby. To her utmost horror she found her drunken husband asleep in the cradle, her daughter squashed beneath the heavy brute. The girl, who had been in good health, was quite dead. The husband remembered nothing of the event, blaming his dipsomania on his wife, who'd created '*a miserable home*'.

TO BE, OR NOT TO BE

Two of the adult deaths involved suicide. No. 3 was pulled out of the canal one Sunday morning. The 41-year-old mother of seven, despite being comparatively well off, had been suffering from depression. She had stayed in bed the whole of the previous day and was joined by her husband at 12.30.a.m. on Sunday morning. One hour later he was awakened by the cries of a policeman, telling him that his wife had been seen climbing out of their window. The husband had locked the doors and hidden the keys as his wife had openly contemplated taking her own life and had turned to drink. She was discovered drowned later that morning.

Alcohol seemed to have played a part in most of the adult deaths. No. 11, the 52-year-old labourer, left a wife and four children. He had previously been sent to prison on three occasions on drink-related charges and was now beginning his fourth stint of three months for stealing a suit whilst under the influence. He could do no more bird and was found hanging from the neck by a warder on his first day inside. Having been in a perpetually drunken state for weeks, self-destruction was the result of his first day of compulsory sobriety.

38. Open fires, alcohol and ignorance were the causes of most domestic accidents. Mothers and children might be pushed onto fires in drunken brawls. The poker was one of the favoured weapons of attack and defence in a domestic. Clothes also caught fire as inebriates, too close to the hearth, dozed off.

Not listed on the chart above, the saddest deaths occurred at the end of April 1871 – those of three girls poisoned in the Crumpsall workhouse. Mary Ann Monaghan 10, Margaret Akroyd 13, and Sarah Ann Royle 18, had been suffering with head colds. Just before going to bed the three girls were given a dose of what a Miss Lees thought was cough mixture prescribed by the surgeon.

A very short time later one of the girls complained of a burning sensation in her throat. Soon all three became completely insensible, emitting deep gasping sounds and writhing around in agony from the excruciating pain of internal burning. A doctor arrived just as Margaret Akroyd, the first and probably the luckiest girl died. His treatment of brandy and an emetic had no beneficial effect on the other two girls, who died agonising deaths one and a half to two hours later. At the Coroner's Court the assistant of the girl's school explained what had happened:

On Saturday night I was very unwell; I went to the cupboard, and on opening it the gaslight shone on the label of Catherine Carnie's medicine, and I immediately put my hand on the next bottle, fully believing that it was the cough mixture, as I always kept them together. I then gave the children a little over one teaspoonful each, but not quite two, that being the quantity of cough mixture I was ordered to give to the big girls. Two of the girls went away. None of them at that time made any complaint. Another girl was in the passage and I poured out a dose for her but she said she had not come for medicine. I had had a bad cough, and I was in the act of raising the glass to my lips, intending to take it myself, when Maria Hughes [the nurse] came in. She had been complaining of a cough, and I said 'Take this Maria, it will do you good. She drank it and immediately said. Oh dear, how it burns my mouth!' Being rather astonished, I turned round to the cupboard, and saw the carbolic acid bottle.

The Coroner suggested to the jury that if Miss Lees was not to be committed for manslaughter the only verdict they could come to was one of 'excusable homicide'.

They found that the three girls had died through misadventure.

However hard some people worked there was never enough money for the basics. Mary Wilson of 22, Copper Street, Rochdale Road was deserted by her husband, who emigrated to the States. She found a job at a costume factory but the pay was so poor – 2s 2d per week in the Summer of 1888 – that she became seriously depressed. Her day started at 8.30. a.m. and she worked solidly until 7.p.m. All she had for sustenance was a little bread and tea. Even strong workers putting in the same hours could only earn 12s per week. Being paid as a piece-worker, Mary found it difficult to toil as quickly as she had done in her younger years. From her pay, 6d. was stopped for cotton and hot water, another 6d. had to be paid back to the forewoman who had lent her money to buy bread. Mary was left with just 1s 2d and her weekly rent was 2s 6d.

Mary threw herself into the canal near Minshull Street in the hope of ending her worries. She was rescued by a dog, which left its master and sprang into the canal to retrieve what George Green, the dog's owner, took to be a bundle of old rags. Aware that attempted suicide was an indictable offence, Mary told the court she fell in accidentally. She was discharged and made straight for the workhouse. The magistrate suggested that the dog be presented with a medal from the Humane Society.

THE SALFORD TRAGEDY

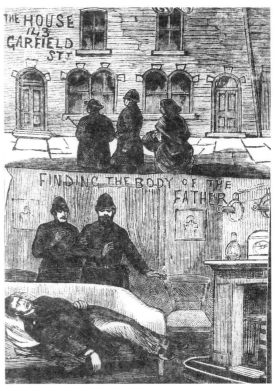

39. The house at the centre of the tragedy in Garfield Street, Salford (1888).

"On climbing to the window I saw a woman and two children in bed. On approaching the bedside I perceived that they were quite dead. I went downstairs and in the kitchen saw the body of Derby on a sofa drawn in front of the fireplace. On a table behind him were some bottles labelled 'Chloral Hydrate' 'Prussic acid' and 'Morphia'. In the front bedroom I discovered four children lying dead in bed. Three were on their right sides with their faces towards the door, and the fourth, the furthest from the door, was lying on its stomach. On searching the lower rooms I found several papers apparently written by the deceased. One paper purported to be the will of the deceased."

40. A break-in was affected following concerns from worried neighbours

Mr. Price had no need to call for silence in the coroner's court, Salford, February 1888. As Police-Constable Shipway methodically read from his notebook, the jurors were visibly numbed, staring blankly before them, their eyes focusing on nothing. Their minds were forming a mental picture of the horrific slaughter discovered in Garfield Street earlier that month. The eight bodies belonged to the entire Derby family: Samuel 36; his wife Ann aged 40; sons Ernest 12, Harold 10 and Frederick 8 and daughters Clare 6, Florence 4 and Gladys 2.

The official role of the inquest was to determine the cause of death, but everybody present was equally as interested as to why such a young family should have had their lives so tragically cut short. The answer was in the papers found at the scene.

Samuel, the father, was not one of the permanently inebriated oafs we read about in most contemporary crime reports. Both he and Ann were teetotal and Samuel was definitely in the top 10% of the population, when judged by his writing skills. The family lived frugally from the savings made in the good times when Sam was a successful businessman. According to the testimony of Samuel's father the hard times had begun some three years previously, when Sam lost his job and seemed to turn in on himself, almost becoming paranoid. He believed there was a conspiracy against him by his brothers and sisters concerning

the will of an Irish relative. Sam felt he'd been swindled out of the property by his own flesh and blood. Sitting at home moping, he became fixated by the supposed injustice, as we shall see.

About a week before the deaths Sam purchased an ounce and a half of syrup of chloral from a chemist, John Cooper, a friend of the Derbys for over 12 years. At the same time he asked the apothecary to witness his will. When questioned as to why the two simultaneous actions did not set alarm bells ringing, Cooper replied that he did not suppose Derby was a man likely to commit suicide. He later told the jury that he knew Derby was in possession of prussic acid, having seen it on a visit to the family home.

On the evening of Monday, 6th February, 12-year-old Ernest was sent to a neighbour's shop with a glass-jar to buy a treat for the whole family: 1lb. of dark treacle. The shopkeeper, Sarah Milner, was the last person to see any member of the family alive again. She would later tell the coroner that that evening she heard sounds of furniture being moved around next door.

Police-Constable Shipway made his gruesome discovery some four days later.

41. P.C. Shipway's first gruesome discovery was of a woman and two children lying in bed. 'They were quite dead'.

Dr. Wilson gave the result of his examination of the dead bodies. Due to their appearance, he concluded that death was caused in all cases by poisoning with prussic acid which, he added, was one of the most painless and deadly poisons known to science. No trace of the poison was found in the bodies, a curious fact Wilson put down to the time lapse between the deaths and his examination. He hypothesised that the lethal acid had been mixed with the treacle and fed to the children by their father. Whether Ann Derby was a party to the tragedy we shall never know.

Sam Derby watched as his wife and the six children he had helped bring into the world left it in convulsions. He himself was not quite ready to meet his maker. He felt terribly wronged and desperately wanted to communicate with those he was to leave behind. A clue to the order of deaths was contained in the postscript Derby added to his will:

My darling wife and children are past the aid of man and I will soon follow.

The fact that the killings were premeditated was obvious from documents and letters found at the scene of crime and posted that day. In one he wrote to his solicitor:

I could not leave my darling wife and children behind. In fact Annie often said she did not want to live after I went, and when I told her a few days ago that I could not stand this any longer, she said she was quite ready to go. I wish our bodies to be sent to Owens college for dissection, or if they are buried, let the funeral be conducted in the quietest way possible, and at the least possible expense.

The coroner would not allow certain letters sent by Derby to his relatives to be read out in court. One, addressed to his sister, was however produced. The jurors listened intently to the spiteful words of a deranged man, who felt himself badly wronged. Given what he would later do, it seems rather hypocritical of Derby to accuse his sister of *'installing poison into others'* :

To my once-loved sister,
By the time this reaches you I shall have gone beyond the reach of your selfish schemes. Had it not been for you and the poison you instilled into others, I believe I might still have had a little happiness in this world. You may now congratulate yourself on the eminent success of your schemes. You will have done with me for ever unless the memory of me haunts you. I don't want to preach to you but if you will take a fool's advice you will begin anew. Your conscience has long been overburdened; don't add to the load – your heartbroken brother.

– "SAMUEL"

Finally Sam calmly mixed a cocktail of prussic acid and chloral hydrate and downed the legal concoction in one quick slug.

The jury found that Samuel Hill Derby murdered his wife and six children. They were also of the belief that he committed suicide while in a state of temporary insanity. Derby had claimed more victims than Jack the Ripper would a few months later.

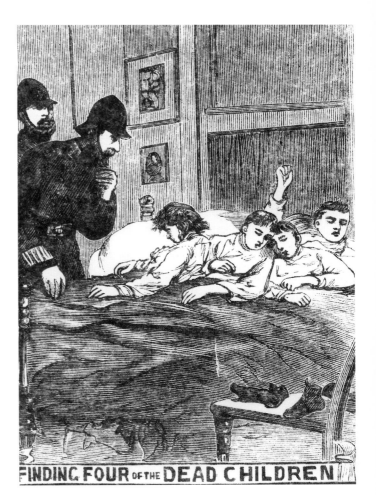

FINDING FOUR OF THE DEAD CHILDREN

42. Samuel Derby was responsible for more deaths than Jack the Ripper later the same year.

Though murder of a loved one followed by suicide, often with a cut-throat razor, was fairly common in Victorian times, the fact that Derby's acts were premeditated and executed by an intelligent, sober man and involved so many young children, deeply shook the whole population of Salford and thousands of people turned out to witness the mass funeral procession, which was reported in the *Manchester City News*:

The funeral of the victims of the tragedy took place on Monday afternoon at the Salford Borough Cemetery. Thousands of people thronged the neighbourhood of Garfield street and from there on to the cemetery the streets were crowded. There were two hearses, each drawn by two black horses. The first of the hearses contained the bodies of Samuel Derby, and his wife, Annie Derby, and the second of those of four of the children... Following the hearses came two private carriages containing relatives and the bodies of the other two children. Afterwards came five other coaches in which were seated the relatives and friends of the deceased, including Mr. Alexander Derby, the father of Samuel Derby, his two brothers and a sister. As the funeral passed along the streets and up through the cemetery hats were raised by the onlookers, and the crowd was for the most part quiet.

HANKY-PANKY IN THE PANTRY

By far the most common occupation for women in Victorian Manchester was that of housewife. In 1871, 52,000 women working as housewives were recorded as unemployed. Cotton mills and the domestic market provided employment for the bulk of unmarried women, with 8,000 girls being employed by each sector. Wages were low in both occupations, but especially so for maids.

Employers believed that because their domestics lived-in, incurring few expenses of their own, there was no need to pay them much more than £12. Not a bad monthly salary for the time, but this was what they could expect for the whole year! Maids were told by the Society for the Promotion of Christian Knowledge not to worry about low wages as serving in a safe, happy home was its own reward.

If a family could not support their children, girls as young as 12 would be pressurised into leaving home and taking up employment at slave labour rates.

Another source of cheap labour was the workhouse. All girls needed were their uniforms, which they usually had to purchase themselves. Some scrimped and saved in other jobs to obtain the money, others had the costs deducted from their meagre salaries. Sometimes charities stepped in, and, by buying wholesale, could kit out a girl for £3. In 1884 this bought: two chemises, one top petticoat, two pairs of drawers, one pair of stays, two nightdresses, two print dresses, one stuff dress, four coarse aprons, four white aprons, two pairs of stockings, one pair of boots, one hat, one jacket, a pair of slippers and the 'good stout box' into which all these were stored.

There was a constant demand for servants, who got their jobs by word of mouth, from employment columns, by placing ads in newspapers, or via one of the many agencies. Ads like the following appeared in local newspapers:

WANTED: AT ONCE, A STRONG GENERAL SERVANT ABOUT 27. ONE WHO CAN WASH. REFERENCE.

WANTED: A GENERAL SERVANT 17 OR 18. NO WASHING. 5, OXFORD ROAD, NEAR THE ARCH.

WANTED AT ONCE: GENERAL SERVANT, 30 TO 40, ABLE TO PLAIN COOK. WAGES 2s. 6d.

WANTED: GENERAL SERVANT TO MIND SMALL HOUSE FOR A GENTLEMAN AND FOUR CHILDREN. £17. COMFORTABLE HOMELY SITUATION. (Manchester Courier 18.5.1888)

Domestic servants wanting places would advertise as follows:

GOOD NURSE AT LIBERTY AGE 14. PROTESTANT.

GOOD COOK AT LIBERTY AGE 36. PROTESTANT.

Many girls soon became disillusioned just days after taking up their posts. A major problem was the unrelieved loneliness. More than half of domestic servants became *maids-of-all-work* – the sole employee. Consequently they had nobody to confide in. The starting salary could be as low as £6 per year. As they grew older, and required more money, they would be replaced by cheaper, younger models.

As we can see from the 1894 timetable below, that of the maid in an upper-middle class Manchester home, there was little time for what we would regard as traditional teenage pursuits. At least this maid, however, had the company of Mr. Simon's cook.

DUTIES OF THE HOUSEMAID

6.45.a.m. Get up. Clean 2 pair' boys' boots.
7.15.a.m. Call boys up and set on cold bath then dust library and lay fire.
7.45.a.m. Dust morning room.
8.00.a.m. Breakfast.
8.30.a.m. Open beds, windows, empty slops.
9.00.a.m. Make beds, dust bedrooms, clean shoes and skirts.
10.00 a.m. Dust bathroom and W.C.. and staircase.
10.30 a.m. Turn out room that is to be cleaned.
1.30.p.m. Lay cloth for lunch.
2.00.p.m. Kitchen dinner.
2.30.p.m. afternoon work.

AFTERNOON WORK

Monday: help cook with the clothes, iron pocket handkerchiefs etc.
Thursday: clean silver.
Saturday: mend bed linen.
4.30.p.m. Schoolroom tea.
6.00.p.m. Lay cloth for dinner; rub up silver and glass.
8.30.p.m. Bring fruit and fresh water.
At dusk light gas, pull down blinds, fasten shutters.

43. A group of Manchester servants. Maids would sometimes be propositioned by the men of the house, seeking a change of diet. Their continued employment might depend on whether the girls spiced up the menu.

44. The girls' dormitory at Salford Union Workhouse. Although appearing austere, conditions were probably better than in many private homes in the area. Girls would leave to marry or take up low-paid jobs in factories or domestic service.

Servants would be housed in cramped attic rooms, which were often cold and draughty. In contrast, kitchen maids had to work in hot, energy-sapping sculleries. Tuberculosis was a continual threat. Many could only afford to change their stockings once a week. Because of the lack of baths, shortage of clothes and poor education, coupled with the heavy, often unhygienic nature of their work (daily emptying of chamber pots etc.) there were frequent complaints of servants being dirty and slovenly. Accordingly, articles of advice frequently appeared in the *Servant's Magazine.* The entry for April 1st 1869 was no joke:

The feet should be washed daily, as well as the armpits, from which an offensive odour is often emitted, unless daily ablution is practised. Cleanliness is next to Godliness.

45. Mary Ellen was sent into service at the age of 12 by her mother as she could no longer afford to feed and clothe her.

The attitude to domestic servants was recognised at the time with an article in the *Manchester City News*, as long ago as 1874, which pointed out:

Many nouveau riche, inconsiderate, selfish, ignorant people have come to look upon the servant as a mere drudging animal.

Given this attitude, perhaps the prototype bed, on show at the Great Exhibition of 1851, should have been put into production. The bed had a clockwork mechanism in one leg which would cause it to collapse at an early hour in the morning dumping the servant onto the floor for the rudest of awakenings.

Many mistresses saw it as their duty to save their servants from temptation. They were expected not to gossip, read sensational stories or lose their tempers. Fraternisation with the opposite sex, though, was viewed as the greatest sin. In 1874, *Cornhill Magazine*, sympathising with the plight of maids, summed up the rules in most households:

No followers, no friends in the kitchen, no laughing to be heard above stairs, no romping for young girls to whom romping is an instinct all the same as with lambs and kittens. No cessation of work except at meal times, no getting out for half an hour into the bright sunshine...

There was no doubt that some *romping* did take place. With no reliable means of birth control maids ran a huge risk if they got up to any hanky panky in the pantry. Not only was there a good chance of falling pregnant amongst the preserves without protection, there was also the near certainty that if this was discovered, they would lose their jobs and be thrown out into the streets.

In reality girls had little chance of flirting other than with the odd delivery boy. They made the most of their little free time of an evening or a Sunday afternoon. The more brazen domestic servants were commonly known as *dollymops* and may have indulged in a little part-time prostitution to make ends meet.

A common contemporary joke, which did the rounds, related to a mistress short of change shouting down the kitchen stairs to her maid:

MISTRESS: *"May, have you any coppers down there?"*

MAID: *"Yes, ma'am, but they are both my cousins."*

One definite hazard of the job was the unsolicited sexual advances of the men of the house, their guests and even their sons. Even today the image of a French maid with feather duster is deemed extremely erotic in certain circles. It seemed even more so in late Victorian England. Many girls had to barricade their doors against male guests. If they did yield it was the girls themselves who were punished, not their seducers.

46. Laura Thompson, lady's maid, c 1910.

47. Edith Paxton, a 21-year-old servant. One of the many underpaid skivvies who supplemented their meagre incomes by a little pilfering.

48. Edith Clarke, a 20-year-old servant, found guilty of stealing from one employer and giving a false reference to another.

49. Ann Williams (4' 6"). A servant who began her official career in crime late in life at the age of 55.

50. Joseph Shaw. The 28-year-old servant would have found it difficult to obtain another post after being convicted of stealing from his employer.

51. Beatrice May Church. The 22-year-old appears terrified of the camera. Another servant accused of giving false references.

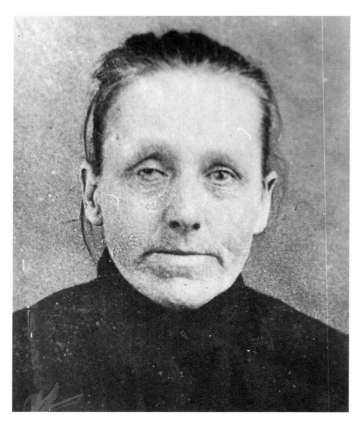

52. Mary Bates, alias Mary Heywood, Florence Birchall and Mary Salway, a notorious thief who gained employment as a servant and stole from her master. Bates would stay just long enough to secrete any valuables and swiftly decamp.

Teenage boys sometimes had their first sexual encounters with *saucy servants*. Walter, in *My Secret Life,* possibly the most pornographic book published in the nineteenth century, had many lusty fantasies about housemaids. As a teenager he was soon putting them into practice. One of the few printable extracts illustrates his obsession:

The servant went to her bed-room, one afternoon; with palpitating heart I followed her, and pushed her on the bed. She was a cheeky, chaffing woman, and guess knew better than I did, what I was about. I recollect her falling back on to the bed, and showing to her knees, 'Oh what lovely legs' said I. 'Nothing to be ashamed of' said she. Whatever my wishes or intentions might have been, I went no further.

If they did fall pregnant many maids tried to abort the child themselves or employed the services of a back-street abortionist. If both methods failed, as they often did, maids would go to extreme lengths to disguise their blooming bodies, and give birth unaided in their pokey attic rooms. If they were to keep their jobs the baby had to be disposed of immediately. The more compassionate sought out baby-farmers, whose fees they could barely afford. The more hard-headed would either kill their baby and dispose of it, or simply leave it unattended. In

1882 Emily Chesworth, an 18-year-old servant from Rusholme, was accused of delivering a baby, not registering it and disposing of its body. Found guilty, Emily was imprisoned for 14 days.

In April 1876, 20-year-old Sarah Ann Jackson, a domestic servant, was charged with the murder of her female child. She had been granted leave by her employer and single-handedly gave birth that same night in March in a house under construction. Her employer knew that she was pregnant and when she returned she asked her what she had done with the baby. Quite casually Sarah told her mistress she had dropped the infant into the *old river* (meaning the river Irwell). She later changed her mind and said she had disposed of it in the Bridgewater canal, where it was later found.

One day earlier Elizabeth McEwan, a domestic servant in the employ of a hairdresser at 97, Stockport Road, Ardwick, gave birth to another girl in a closet at the rear of the premises. She had only been employed for three days and, wishing to keep her job, threw her daughter into an ashpit – partially covering her with ashes. Her employer, a Mr. Brown, sensing something was amiss, followed her. They crossed in an alleyway. Brown continued to walk towards the ashpit and heard a weak cry. Jumping into the foul-smelling human waste he dragged the baby out. Somehow she was still clinging to life but died at the police-station a short time later.

Harsh though life was in domestic service, there was always a roof over one's head and four meals a day. These 'luxuries' were envied by some women, who, having children, were therefore unable to find employment in service. One desperate woman made the ultimate sacrifice. She murdered her twelve-month old baby daughter in order to obtain employment *below stairs*.

In the winter of 1865 Mary Bibby resided in Salford with her daughter and Mary's 11-year-old sister, Ann. Mary was desperate to escape the biting cold and constant hunger pangs. The sole obstruction preventing her from going into service lay in her arms, doped with laudanum. Desperate people resort to desperate measures and Mary

53. However harsh the conditions in domestic service, the alternatives of factory work, the workhouse or marriage to a brutal husband were often worse.

determined to rid herself of what she saw as the mill-stone around her neck.

On January 8th, Mary took a box, fastened with cord, to Victoria station. The only writing on the package read **'Mrs. Clegg, passenger from Manchester to Preston'**. She gave the parcel to the guard on a train going to the said destination but did not board herself.

When not recovered the box was sent to Fleetwood, back to Preston and on to Euston. After some days in the left-luggage department the box was opened. On 4-5 inches of straw, lying on the left side with knees doubled up, lay the remains of baby Ada, her body now of a deep red hue. A deathly reverent hush fell over the office as railway workers crossed themselves. The baby was buried at Finchley cemetery.

Quite how police traced the dead baby back to Mary is unclear. Little police time was spent following up such cases. It seemed that an extremely conscientious officer of the law sought to resolve the question of the baby's identity. The obvious place to start was Manchester, where the sad journey had begun.

Mary had told her sister that Ada had gone to stay with her aunt in Yorkshire. She was informed, in no uncertain terms, that if she did not tell neighbours this version of events she would have her throat cut! It was probably one of these suspicious neighbours who alerted the authorities about the disappearance of the baby. Ann, Mary's sister, was invited down to London to identify her disinterred niece. Death had been caused by suffocation.

When arrested Mary protested her innocence:

"What, murder my poor Ada? No, never, but God is above the devil!"

After just 40 minutes Mary Bibby was found guilty of manslaughter.

Sad cases similar to the above were thankfully not nearly as common as the numerous cases of pilfering. Employers had to take a gamble when hiring staff. References were often forged and some maids stayed just long enough to relieve the home owner of a few prize possessions. Small scale pilfering was fairly common and traps to test a servant's honesty were sometimes set. Coins would deliberately be left under furniture for the maid to 'discover'. Her job often depended on whether she reported or pocketed the find.

Those sacked or those who refused to work for a pittance sometimes turned to prostitution. In 1860 Arthur Mursell, a clergyman, condemned the low wages paid to servants in Manchester. He claimed they were responsible for girls walking the streets to supplement pay, many eventually becoming full-time prostitutes. Indeed once servants had swapped jobs their lives changed drastically from cleaning, church-going and chastity to shopping, supping and sex.

Some girls applying for jobs in domestic service never lifted a duster in anger. Advertisements were placed in the domestic service columns by brothel owners and traffickers in the white slave trade. Girls were ushered off to the continent and not told the true nature of their position until arrival. Servants were reliant upon their box of clothes as much as the artisan his tools. If they were cajoled into a house of ill-repute, these boxes might be withheld by the brothel bully. Girls could not take their pick, if they were unable to open their boxes they had to take the money. When girls fell upon hard times they might sell their clothes and therefore make themselves unemployable.

Harsh though their lives were, many servants preferred their lot to that of married and unmarried mothers who seemed to be forever pregnant and spent much of their lives bearing and rearing large, often sickly, families.

LONELINESS, LAUDANUM AND LAUNDRY

54. *'Exhibit No.1 your honour.' One of the many victims of child neglect. Young children were sometimes seen as an inconvenience, often left under the supervision of a brother or sister not much older than themselves.*

With women being deemed unsuitable for most jobs, other than child-bearing and caring, the career opportunities for young ladies did not appear over-attractive in 19th century Manchester. Most women wed and were officially listed as unemployed. The childhood dreams of some young married girls soon turned into a living nightmare, played out with brutish husbands who drank a large percentage of the weekly earnings and often flew into a rage when there was no supper on the table. Over the years many women lost their looks, their strength and even their will to live, following the birth and death of large numbers of babies. Life for many was just one long round of loneliness, laudanum and laundry.

Unwanted pregnancies were probably the greatest problem encountered by Victorian women. As we have seen, employers would not hire domestic servants with babies. Those mothers who worked in the mills and factories would have to pay baby-farmers or elderly neighbours to care for their offspring. Sometimes babies were left under the supervision of an older sister, who might be as young as eight. The children too, had to be fed and clothed, and more often than not, given medicine. The financial strain was too much for some mothers and many tried to induce abortions. They often enlisted the help of so-called experts, but on occasions the terminations did not result in one death but two.

Whilst infant life seemed so cheap, those found guilty of attempting to procure an abortion were given comparatively stiff sentences for the times. In 1871, 29-year-old Lydia Smith was sentenced to seven years for 'attempting to cause the miscarriage of one Emily Smith'.

A more serious case came before the courts four years later. Alfred Heap, a chemist and quack doctor had, for a fee of £1, terminated the pregnancy of Margaret McKivett, a confectioner living in Hyde road. Margaret died from the effects of the operation. Having already served five years for a similar offence, Heap was sentenced to death. Despite the jury's recommendation of mercy, Heap was hanged in Liverpool, his last words were to God: 'Receive my soul'.

For those whose attempts at abortion failed immediate infanticide was a second option. Unwanted babies had their lives terminated in a variety of ways. Several methods involving buckets of water, umbilical cords and pricking with needles were employed, and the baby officially listed as stillborn.

55. Children at the Crumpsall Workhouse Infirmary, for some the first years of a lifetime in institutions.

Many were simply abandoned in poorly lit, least frequented areas of the city, their little bodies discovered by policemen or human scavengers. They would be found in a rag, a piece of sacking or naked, never in properly made garments. The indifference to this human suffering was displayed by the kind of off-hand, curt reports typified by this item in the Manchester City News, October 1, 1864:

There was the inquest on the body of a new born female infant, which was found lying dead between some stones on Ducie-bridge on Wednesday morning. The child had been born alive, and a verdict of wilful murder against some persons unknown was returned.

In 1864 Catherine Lalley left her illegitimate 10-day-old daughter to die in a dung heap in Dog-Kennel lane, Willington. She was traceable only because the baby had been born in a workhouse where records were kept.

Other infants were unashamedly murdered and dumped, the perpetrators hoping that the baby could not be identified. In most cases the perpetrators literally got away with murder as in the following typical case in 1888.

BABY MURDER IN MANCHESTER

The adjourned inquest on the body of a newly-born female child, which was discovered on Friday in a pail taken from Scotland Bridge-yard, Red Bank, was held on Monday. It was given in evidence at the previous sitting that the child had been born alive, but that it had been subjected to violence which had led to its death, the nostrils and front of the neck bearing the marks of a person's thumb and finger. There was no evidence of identification and the inquest was adjourned so that the police might make further inquiries.

A verdict of wilful murder by person or persons unknown was returned.

When arrests were made, sentences varied from complete discharge, to a few months or years for manslaughter, to execution for murder. In 1875 17-year-old Jane Lloyd concealed the birth of a child – born out of wedlock – and disposed of the body. Pleading guilty, a lenient Judge discharged her.

In 1896, John Hirst, 26, a bricklayer from Chorlton-on-Medlock, told the court he had become tired of his baby daughter. His solution to the problem was simple – as others do with unwanted kittens, so he did with his own daughter. He strangled her and threw her into the canal. The callous apology for a human being was hanged on August 4th, 1896.

Not all cases were so brutal or clear-cut. Some babies died from inappropriate care.

BABY-FARMERS

In 1868 a Physician wrote to the Salford Weekly News voicing his concern about baby farmers:

Factory workers marry very early, and, as female 'hands' can earn nearly as much as their husbands, the babies of these young couples are left, not infrequently, in the entire charge of old women who take care of as many children, legitimate and illegitimate, as they can get. The charge for this taking care of a child appeared to vary from eighteenpence to three shillings a week.

Numerous were the cases of chronic diarrhoea and atrophy from Mesenteric disease in these nursed children that were brought to the hospital. Some of the nurses were women of dissolute habits and without shame; others, feeble women, so old as to be in their second childhood. Few of the nursed children came to the hospital for trifling maladies, the majority were brought when the nurse believed that the child was so near death that a doctor's certificate would be wanted. The diseases from which the farmed children suffered could be traced in nearly all cases to the improper food that has been systematically given to the child; in some cases, to the insufficiency of the quantity of food, and to the free use of 'quieting stuff'. Children but a few months old were fed by the less indifferent of these baby-farmers with some of their own coarse food; while others, who were in the charge of the worse section of nurses received little else but bread, water, potatoes and (to keep them quiet) a little coarse sugar which they sucked through muslin and other rags...

It was difficult to prove wilful neglect on the part of baby farmers but three years later, in a case which was to become the talk of women from all walks of life, the prosecution attempted to do just that in the trial of Frances Rogers.

56. The only love some children ever knew was that for a rag doll.

57. Children were often left in the charge of old women or plied with laudanum, sold at that time by any grocer or market trader. Chronic diarrhoea and atrophy were the consequences of the habit and poor diet.

FRANCES ROGERS

In 1871, an urgent loud prolonged knocking and shaking of the door at 156, Knightley Road, Queens Road, was followed a few seconds later with the command to open up. Frances Rogers, a middle-aged woman, was going about her usual domestic chores that Sunday afternoon. It was the knock she had always feared. She knew from the authoritarian tone that this was no social call. She cast a quick worried look over the spartan room furnished, here and there, with emaciated children cuddling sickly looking babies. The second rapping was even louder and Frances reluctantly half-opened the door, filling the gap with her body so the visitors might not see inside,

Two curt police officers, of the no-nonsense school, brushed her aside, telling her they wanted to search the premises. Frances confirmed that her name was Rogers but when asked if her husband was at home made no reply. Deathly pale and trembling, she followed the officers as they poked their noses into unwashed rooms and grimy cupboards. She answered questions as to the identity of the sparsely clad and diseased children and babies cowering in the corners.

In the kitchen a boy about 9-years-old was holding a male baby about nine months, to his chest. The infant was pathetically sucking at the tube of a feeding bottle but there was no bottle attached. Frances told the officers that she had taken in the baby for 4 shillings per week. On the table were the remains of a small loaf, a little mutton, a jug containing some milk mixed with water (mostly water) and a small bottle of laudanum.

Frances warily followed the officers up the rotting stairs. The group entered a back bedroom, which was completely unfurnished save for a pile of straw serving as a bed. Here an 8-year-old girl was doing her best to nurse an eight-week-old female baby. They were discovered shivering under a damp, old woollen blanket and sodden shirt. The baby had been living there for a few days and was being farmed by Frances Rogers for a fee of 5 shillings a week.

There were no beds in the house, just straw and a torn parasol. One of the few items of furniture was in the parlour. On the sofa the trio came across a man in his shirt-sleeves halfway through his Sunday lunchtime jug of beer. Edward James told the police he had been living with Frances for just two weeks.

Frances began praying under her breath, 'God, please let them go now… please!'

Frances's prayers were not answered, for at this point the police chose to inspect the cellar. As the policemen examined some dirty nappies discarded under a window sill, Frances covertly made her way to the darkened side of the cellar. With her back deliberately turned to the officers she began fumbling with what the police first thought was a pile of dirty rags. The damp cellar immediately filled with an overpowering stench so strong the officers had to mask their mouths and noses as they felt their Sunday lunches re-surface. When questioned, Frances blamed the smell on a dog they used to keep. The trio quickly made their way as best they could to the relatively sweet air of the kitchen. Frances was carrying a coal bag and *dirty napkins*. The cellar's stench had somehow followed then up the stairs and invaded the kitchen, where it had not been noted before. The policemen pulled up some floorboards but found nothing. The stench seemed to be coming from under the dress of Frances Rogers, who had adopted an awkward pose, as if concealing something next to her body. Despite her protestations one of the officers put his hand up

Frances's skirt and pulled out a paper parcel – the source of all the foul air. When opened the decomposing remains of a baby boy were laid bare on the kitchen floor.

"*Oh dear, I know nothing about it*," was all Mrs. Rogers offered by way of explanation. Edward James, who had joined the small group, also denied all knowledge of the stinking parcel, which was later proven to have been in the cellar for about ten days.

Both adults were taken to the police station. In a preliminary hearing a surgeon testified that the baby, probably about 6-7 months old, had died after a sudden deprivation of food, having previously been well-fed. Both Frances Rogers and Edward James were charged with murdering one child and attempting to murder others. The City Police court was packed with spectators, nearly all women, who showed great interest in the case.

Although traces of opium were found in the dead boy's body, death was adduced to have been caused by convulsions following starvation. The two live babies found in the house had been examined. The girl, at three months, was not as well developed as she should have been, and the boy, at six months, was positively and dangerously

58. The survivors. The infant mortality rate in Manchester was amongst the worst in the country.

59. Some children survived and prospered against all odds.

emaciated. His eyes were red and sunk into his head, the face very wan and he cried continuously.

A chemist from 714, Rochdale Road testified that he had sold Frances Rogers laudanum every morning (except Sundays) over the previous five weeks. She paid a penny for between 90 and 100 drops on the pretext that she wanted it for toothache.

Next to testify were the mothers of the two sick babies found in the house. With the proceedings being so sensitive they did not wish to be identified. Both names and addresses were withheld and one woman, aged about 22, was examined in private as the magistrates were informed that she might suffer

'severe consequences' if examined in open court.

Both mothers had agreed to pay Rogers five shillings each week. It appears that the baby-farmer had lied about her domestic arrangements but in her defence both mothers agreed that their babies were in a poorly condition when they handed them over. At the time of the trial both infants were being cared for in the workhouse infirmary, where they were just clinging to life.

Edward James had been telling the truth. He was just one of a number of transients who shared lodgings with Frances Rogers and had nothing to do with her business. He was discharged.

The crown openly admitted that there would

have been no charges brought but for the fact that Frances Rogers had placed three advertisements in newspapers. They argued that she 'adopted' the babies and simply allowed them to starve, doping them with laudanum when their hungry screams became too much to bear. After much legal argument the charge was reduced to manslaughter. The sentence passed – 20 years – was extremely severe for the time and nature of the crime.

Frances Rogers was far from being the only child minder to administer laudanum. Indeed daily doping of children seemed to be the rule rather than the exception.

Three druggists in Deansgate stated that in 1871 alone, they supplied a staggering 1,260 families with weekly supplies of opiates. A select committee on the protection of infant life was alerted to the problem:

Of the really poorer classes I may safely say there is scarcely a single family in which the practice [of giving drugs to children to keep them docile] does not prevail: the way it is done is this. The mother goes out to her work in the morning, leaving her child in charge either of a woman who cannot be troubled with it, or with another child of perhaps, ten years old.

A dose of 'quietness' is therefore given to the child to prevent it being troublesome; the child thus drugged sleeps and may waken at dinner time; so when the mother goes out again the child receives another dose; well the mother and father come home at night quite fatigued, and as they must rise early to begin work for the day, they must have sleep undisturbed by the child so it is again drugged, and in this manner young children are often drugged three times in each day.

Short spells inside may have come as a welcome break for some mothers.

ALL STICK AND NO CARROT

Between 1790 and 1868 tens of thousands of the criminal population did some bird in New Bayley Gaol. When the prison was first designed and built, most serious offenders were either being transported or hanged. By the time of New Bayley's demolition in 1872, the prison system had changed beyond all recognition. The only constant was that the regime was harsh, and with the introduction of the tread wheel and crank, some offenders, if asked, might have preferred a trip to the colonies.

New Bayley was a short-term prison, with offenders sometimes serving sentences as short as three days. In 1847-8 over 90% of inmates had been sentenced to less than six months, for a variety of petty offences ranging from theft, to drunkenness and prostitution. Just over 2% were serving more than three years. Prisoners convicted of the most serious offences, once transportation was abolished, were sent to gaols like Preston.

What is today termed 'a short, sharp shock' was probably too short and certainly no shock to the regular clientele of New Bayley. For some drunkards the three days were used, like some health farms today, for drying out, with the additional bonus of not picking up a hefty tab at the end of their stay. The Chaplain's report of 1857 observes:

The prisoner often reaches us in the evening of the first day; is well washed the second, and turned out the following morning at 7 a.m., making gaol a little more than a public bath.

Three day stayers were probably the biggest problem for turnkeys, no sooner had the guests learned the ropes (oakum picking) than they were released again.

Life inside for longer periods was summed up by one inmate as 'hard work, hard fare and a hard bed.' In the male prison the solitary cells were 7' 3" long and 5' 9" wide. The walls were over 20" thick. Three-bedded cells measured 12' 4" by 7' 4". Cells for refractory prisoners were even smaller, unheated and so damp that even the cold-hearted prison authorities allowed those under punishment back to the relative luxury of their own cells at night.

Offences requiring internal discipline included: jumping off the tread wheel; quarrelling; bartering food and introducing tobacco. There was quite a trade in the weed, which was often thrown over prison walls by friends of the inmates.

Because of the large turnover of prisoners it was almost impossible to enforce the rule of silence. Besides being sent to freeze in the punishment cells, meagre food rations would also be stopped.

Although New Bayley would never have made the lists in any Good Food Guide there were those outside who envied the prisoners their regular meals, however spartan and rotten. Men were allowed 20 oz of brown bread daily. This was 24 hours old and broken into three pieces to be served with breakfast, lunch and supper. One half oz of salt would also accompany the meals. Breakfast and supper consisted of 1 quart of oatmeal gruel, made from 2.5 oz of oatmeal to each quart. There was some variation at dinner. Two days a week inmates dined upon half a pound of beef and one pound of potatoes.

On another two days per week, one quart of pea soup was served. The vegetarian regime continued with one and a half pounds of potatoes making up the main meal on the other two working days. On Sundays prisoners feasted on a quart of stew.

Female prisoners received 16 oz of bread; half an ounce of salt; 1 quart of gruel, morning and evening and one pint of stew with 1lb. of boiled potatoes for dinner every day. The stew for males was made with one cow's head for every twenty prisoners and for the females one cow's head to every forty.

Male prisoners were rigged out in grey woollen suits which consisted of a cap, jacket, waistcoat and trousers without pockets. Other clothes included a linen shirt, stockings, clogs and surprisingly, given the heightened suicide risk, a stock (or neckchief) and belt. Female prisoners donned a wrapper, petticoat of woollen body linen and stays *'if usually worn'*.

There was almost no heating anywhere in the prison and prisoners were also forced to wash in cold water. There were no baths beyond the first, at reception. Men were expected to shave at least once a week and keep their hair *'decently short'*. Towels, brown soap and combs were provided.

With fewer and fewer colonies willing to accommodate the misfits of British society, prisons throughout the country started experiencing problems of overcrowding. By the 1840s three hammocks were being strung up in cells intended for just one inmate. Each cell contained a night bucket. The W.C.s in communal prison areas consisted of slate urinals and privies, which discharged straight into the river Irwell.

The diet and overcrowded conditions at New Bayley led to many visits to the prison doctor with both feigned and genuine illness. Amongst the most common reported illnesses were *'low fevers, Itch, Venereal and constipated bowels.'* Predictably, prisoners went to extraordinary lengths to feign illness as a short respite from the gruelling everyday grind.

The bell rang at 6.a.m. and prisoners began work at 6.30 a.m. Breakfast like all meals was taken in shifts, between 8 and 9, with one half-hour being allowed. The daily service in the chapel started at 11.a.m. – the only official location where male and female prisoners might see each other. One hour was allowed for dinner at sometime between 11.30. and 1 p.m.. Prisoners were expected to stagger their hour for supper to between 4 and 7. At all other times detainees were expected to work. At 7 p.m. the bell rang, the final roll call given and inmates locked away for the night. In winter, hours were shorter – about 7.5 per day. Thus was the lot for inmates, the drudgery only being relieved on Sundays, Christmas, Good Friday, days of fasting and thanksgiving.

Most prison labour served very little purpose. The tread-wheel, which was introduced to New Bayley in 1824, was initially only used by men and boys. In the summer it would accommodate up to 80 prisoners at one time. The height of each step was just over eight inches. There were two complete revolutions per minute. In summer roughly half the prison population trod the boards. In winter the numbers at any one time increased to 96, with over 75% of the prison population participating, in unison, in the daily uphill march.

Initially used for rasping logwood, the power generated by the treadmill, was harnessed to grind sand after 1841. Subsequently it was disconnected and *'drove the air'*. Fat or tall men and heavy drinkers suffered most on the tread wheel and would sometimes throw themselves off, preferring the punishment of solitary confinement. Younger boys seemed to be able to handle the 'work' best, although they were constantly being admonished for chattering to each other. Use of the tread wheel in the New Bayley was restricted after 1841.

Other prison jobs included: weaving, winding, wool-picking, hair-picking, rope-making, pin-heading, clogging, shoemaking, tailoring, cabinet making, painting, gardening etc.

The Reverend J.E. Mercer, the chaplain of New Bayley, 1856, appears to have been something of a misogynist. In his report on the work women did he notes:

The hard labour in this prison consists of the mangle and the wash tub. The crank, which is nothing more than a continuous mangle… would seem a proper labour to them… it would help check women who cannot be employed in the wash-house, and who instead assail the officers with the most abominable and filthy language.

Although outnumbered by roughly three to one, women caused the authorities more than their fair share of problems. Here's the Reverend Mercer again, commenting on the women's lives prior to sentencing:

more degraded than the men, more drunken, idle and depraved… [They] sit round the fire all day, inert and listless (smoking their clay pipes).

Quite how the Reverend acquired this privileged insight into their lives is not made clear but he went on to attack the imprisoned prostitutes saying that in Angel Street 46 of the 54 houses were brothels!

A report published earlier in 1843, significantly *not* by a man of the church, was more sympathetic to female prisoners:

The females who have been prostitutes, are less reclaimable than male offenders. One of the most beautiful women I ever beheld, a prostitute, was repeatedly convicted of theft, and at last transported. She told me on her departure that all

60. *An early policeman before the introduction of helmets. Many of those arrested by this P.C. would have spent a few days or weeks in the New Bayley.*

the young women she had known, in the same line as herself, had been transported, and that she had long expected it.

The most depraved women we have are from Liverpool. One woman has been here 200 times within the last 6 years! She comes here generally to recruit her health. Another has been here 50 times, and cried when she was last discharged.

The crank, used by both sexes, was probably more detested than the tread wheel. Between 9,000 and 12,000 rotations were expected per day and the number of whippings increased after its introduction in 1831. Though no women were flogged after 1820, they were punished by being handcuffed or put into a straight jacket.

Most prisons were nearly all stick and very little carrot. Attempts were made to educate the prison population but the syllabus, in the hands of religious zealots, appeared so dull that some young people may have been put off learning to read for life. In 1843 the first lessons in instruction were to learn the Lord's Prayer, the Creed, the Ten Commandments and their duty towards God and their neighbour. Instruction was interrupted by the relatively short school term, usually the few weeks of the original sentence.

In 1861, of the 681 boys and girls entering the prison, 51 could not read a letter; 8 were incapable of learning; 519 could not read the New Testament intelligibly and only 17 could read well. On discharge, we are told, 219 could miraculously read the New Testament well; 93 were good readers and 369 as illiterate as before.

THE LAST EXECUTION

In 1864, following the opening of the Manchester Assizes, the New Bailey became a hanging prison. In total six men were left dangling at the end of a rope in three separate public executions. The stringing up of three Fenians – the Manchester Martyrs – in 1867 caused such outrage amongst the Irish population throughout the country that security forces were put on full alert and thousands of temporary volunteers recruited in case of an uprising.

The last public execution in Salford was a double bill, attracting spectators from far and wide. The supporting act was a man named Faherty who, because a Mary Hanmer continually spurned the drunkard's advances, on Christmas Day 1867, struck the 36-year-old about the head with a poker. The five lethal blows were delivered in Droylesden. Poor Mary received the sort of Christmas box no-one would want.

The other felon, hanged with Faherty, was Miles Weatherhill, known as the Todmorden murderer. Most of the crowd had come to see him take his final jump. Miles Weatherill had fallen for the charms of one Jane Smith, a servant girl at Todmorden Parsonage. He held a grudge against the family for not allowing him to visit, and then dismissing his girlfriend. Armed with a pistol and poker, and somewhat surprisingly a Bible, he set out on a bloody mission of revenge. Breaking into the Parsonage he wounded or killed anybody, including the servants, who got in his way. This was one crime that could not be blamed on the demon drink, the angry young man was completely sober.

The double execution was witnessed by a reporter from the *Salford Weekly News*:

…The crowd which had been very dense in New Bailey street, from about six o'clock until ten or half past, on Friday night thinned off rapidly after that time, and by midnight comparatively few members were in the street. At two o'clock in the morning the numbers had sensibly augmented, but did not probably exceed a couple of hundred, the majority being on the Stanley-street side of the gallows. They were chiefly rough lads, who had taken up their positions behind, or where possible, upon the barriers nearest the drop, with the evident intention of maintaining the vantage ground to the last, and satisfying their morbid curiosity to the utmost possible extent. There was a more than usual proportion of the weaker sex, even at that early hour. Though as yet numerically small, the crowd was extremely demonstrative. They were evidently in the best of spirits and bent on enjoying themselves after their own fashion. A continuous fire of coarse jokes were directed from barrier to barrier; peals of laughter, in which the shrill treble of females was conspicuous, bearing testimony to the more effective sallies of wit.

At frequent intervals snatches of popular songs were roared out lustily – an admiring audience taking up the chorus with tremendous gusto. The musical programme was varied, if not choice. The favourite compositions appeared to be 'I wish I was a swell' 'He's a pal o' mine' 'John Barleycorn' 'Rule Britannia' and something consisting of 'Oh Jerusalem'…

At seven o'clock the thong was estimated at about ten thousand. It was easy to see that it included a large proportion of the ruffianly element, although the ruffianism was in its most amiable mood. Deansgate and the back slums of Manchester and Salford had sent their swarms of spectators; there were shoals of dissipated looking lads and youths, the closely cropped hair of many of whom suggested acquaintance with the scissors of some prison barber. Dirty looking women and factory girls still formed a notable feature in the scene…*

By half-past seven the mob covered the whole of New Bailey street, and extended beyond at each end as far as the eye could reach from the neighbourhood of the drop. The density of the crowd continued steadily to increase and before the time of execution arrived there would be not less than from 20,000 to 25,000 persons present…

Shortly before 8 o'clock, the hour of execution, the procession started, and, headed by the undersherrif accompanied by the gaol authorities and officials, slowly made its way to the scaffold. Faherty came first, attended by the Rev. Father Gadd, then followed Weatherill with the Rev. Mr. Caine… Neither required any support. Faherty walked with a measured slow step, and showed no outward sign of the agitation he had undergone, except that the hue of death was already on his countenance, and his eyes were fixed on vacancy with a glassy stare, as if he was unconscious of everything, although he mechanically and audibly repeated the responses of the church and the priest. Weatherill had not changed. He looked the same fresh complexioned youth who excited at his trial, if not sympathy, at least surprise and regret that one so young, possessing so much the outward appearance of innocence and self-restraint should be guilty of so great a crime. His eye was as intelligent as ever, and he walked with a steady, elastic step…

At the sounding of the prison clock, the strokes of which were distinctly heard, the rustling motion of the multitude settling itself down for the coming spectacle appealed to the eye and ear with equal effect. As the door opened the appearance of those pale-faced thousands straining with expectation was a sight far more awful than the gallows itself. Faherty was the first to appear… He turned once to the right and once to the left, as if in mechanical obedience to an officer's order, and then, as if bewildered by the host of staring faces, he turned his eyes to the sky, and did not again alter the direction of his gaze. The motion of his lips, distinctly seen at a considerable distance from the scaffold, showed with what fervour he followed the Rev. Father Gadd in the prayers appointed to be read at the hour of death. During the dreadful delay which occurred while Calcraft was knotting one end of the rope round the wretched man's neck and throwing the other end in the folds round the beam, and then leisurely forming the loop, the crowd

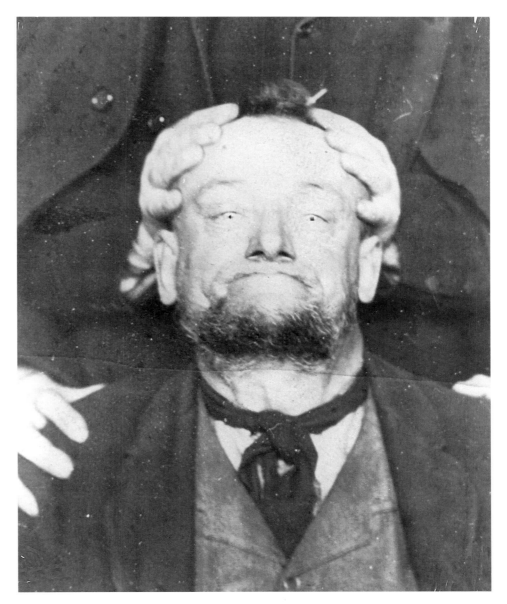

61. William Allen served time in the New Bayley after being convicted of stealing a carpet in 1863. Here photographed in 1895, a little gentle persuasion was needed so that he could no longer pass himself off with the aliases of Hallam and Jackson.

showed a natural impatience at the executioner failing to make short work of his revolting office…

Faherty still seemed quite unconscious of everything around him, except the presence of the priest and the approach of death. He was dressed in apparently a new suit of black clothes, and carried at his breast a conspicuously bright gold cross, attached to a broad blue ribbon, round his neck. When Calcraft at length drew the cap over his head, Faherty's outward firmness seemed to be deserting him, he was left waiting for his doom as one who but usurps his life.

At a signal from Calcraft, the Rev. Mr. Caine and Miles Weatherill appeared in view. The sight of the Todmorden murderer seemed to strike the crowd with a new and entirely different sensation. There was an instantaneous buzz of recognition, not only of the man himself, but of his strangely appalling crime and his desperately incurred punishment. He,

too, was attired in a suit of deep black, and showed the same neatness of personal appearance that struck the observers of him at his trial. He walked with a firm step, and his face, though it showed a death-like pallor, wore a singularly solemn expression. From the time he came in sight until the cap was drawn over his head, he kept his eyes, which seemed strikingly large and prominent, fixed upwards, and he never once glanced at the crowd. The multitudinous sound of half-hushed voices grew in depth and volume and the executioner proceeded with his work. Prayers were audibly offered that God would have mercy on the wretched youths' souls and the stifled cries of the women were pitiable to hear. The spectacle was sufficient to move the most hardened. In compliance with his fervently-expressed wish, Weatherill was permitted to hold in his hand, the prayer-book found in his possession when he was

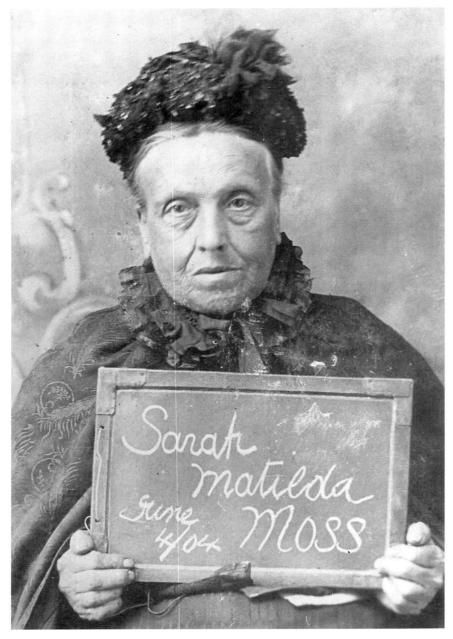

62. Sarah Moss, a regular at the New Bayley. Her first conviction was in 1852. Between 1852-108 she spent 31 years in prison, mostly for stealing shawls.

first arrested, and which he appeared to have carried about with him while he was meditating and even committing his terrific crime. Neither of the men attempted to speak.

Everything being in readiness, Calcraft hurriedly quitted the platform, and before one could again draw breath there was a clank of iron and a thud of timber and all was over. There was no symptom of disorder in the crowd, the only sounds at the last were the peculiar gasps of sensation, as the successive stages of the awful ceremony were accomplished and the sudden wailing of women as it concluded.

The bodies were cut down at nine o' clock and buried during the afternoon in the same place as the Fenian convicts.

Calcraft, the hangman, later revealed that he had received a threatening letter informing him that he would be shot at 8.a.m., the hour of the execution, in revenge for the Fenian hangings of the previous year.

The New Bayley closed in 1868 and was replaced by Strangeways. A newspaper article in that year, when jurors visited an unnamed prison, noted that prisoners carrying cans of water in the yard for the cooking department immediately put down the cans when they saw the visitors and *'stood with their faces thrust to the wall'*. Such was the rigour of the discipline in force. The New Bayley, demolished in 1872, was immortalised in the following verse:

NEW BAYLEY TREAD-MILL

In Manchester New Bayley
We've got a new corn mill
Aud those whose actions send them here,
Of it will have their fill:
Prisoners let this a caution be,
Obey me in a crack,
Or I will take my whip and flog
You right well o'er your back.
So work, work, mind, mind,
And work with free good will,
In Manchester New Bayley
We've got a treading mill.
At six o'clock the bell does ring,
To work we must proceed,
To turn this plaguy treading mill
Would kill a horse indeed:
If you should give him one black look
Or offer to rebel,
He'd keep a Tommy every day,
And march you in the cell.
Those may call this a cruel plan
Who are not fond of work,
But while you're here you must become
As nimble as a cork.
Pull off your coat and try your strength,
What you can undergo;
O dear, this cursed treading mill
It makes me puff and blow.
If I work three months at this mill
I fear I shall be dead,
I feel the flesh desert my bones,
I wish I had been wed.
Had I a wife, a very good wife,

She'd pity my sad case,
And by some means she'd teach me
To keep from such a place.
We prisoners here are bound,
And cannot once say nay;
This is a place of exercise,
Therefore we must obey:
If you attempt for to neglect,
The consequence we tell,
You'll get the whip across your back,
And lodge in the black cell.
Your conversation makes me quake
And tremble with great fear,
My collar bone will surely break,
I wish I'd not come here:
The d___I take your collar bone,
Your idle bones beside;
Mind your work or you will get
The lash across your hide.
When these treadles you come to tread
Mind how you make your steps,
For if your foot should come to slip,
You'd get a smack i'th chops;
Besides, your skilly they will stop,
And nothing you must fetch,
You'll ramble about in your clogs,
Just like a forlorn wretch.
So recollect I caution you,
Beware of our strong nets;
For dainties we do not preserve,
To stuff a prisoner's guts:
If ever I get my discharge,
I'll labour with good will,
And no more taste of Manchester
New Bayley's Treading-Mill.

THE NEW REGIME

Strangeways, with accommodation for 744 men and 315 women, opened its doors for business in June 1868. Those old lags who had experienced conditions in the New Bayley would have rated it a couple of stars above their old haunt in any good prison guide. Equipped with W.C.s, a water tap and gas lighting in each cell, conditions were better than many prisoners had ever seen.

In an average week in 1871 the prison population numbered 629. Of these 302 were employed in profitable labour: mat weaving, sewing, knitting and oakum picking; 114 short term prisoners or summary offenders drove the tread wheel or turned the crank; 129 were employed in various tasks about the prison and 84 not employed.

Internal discipline was re-enforced with corporal punishment, a reduction in the already meagre diet or a short stay in the punishment cells. The most dreaded was the cat. Graphic tales of prison life were related by the inmates themselves.

The following account of a flogging was related by a reformed criminal who had done his fair share of breech-buzzing (pocket-picking) but vehemently denied the charge of garrotting for which he was sentenced. In the 1860's the anonymous career criminal, small, slim and quick-witted, received a seven-stretch and two dozen lashes. Following two, carefully calculated weeks of agonising wait, the day of punishment arrived:

A SCRATCHING IN STRANGEWAYS

I was led from the cell into the yard and stripped to my trousers. It was as cold as could be, for it was in December, and I shivered and felt just as bad as ever I did in my life. I was taken to a wall and saw two rings in the bricks about as high as my shoulders and two posts of wood, standing a bit apart and away from the rings, with a cross piece that seemed as if it could slide up and down. At the bottom of the posts was a kind of box with two round holes in the top. They opened this like you might pull a drawer out of a cupboard, and I was made to stand in it.

My feet were fitted into the corners and then they closed it and screwed it up. My legs were just fixed in the holes now up to over the knee, and I was as fast as in a vice. My hands were put into the rings and the cross-piece of wood fitted across my chest by the doctor. I was as tight as a drum, and my back was a little bent and forced out and my arms stretched full length. I couldn't bend my knees or shift about in any way…

One of the screws had got the cat in his hand, and he was a big fellow, but not half a bad 'un. He said to me he hoped I shouldn't think any worse of him for it, but if he didn't do it some 'un else would. Of course it was his duty, but he did lay it on.

The doctor stood by with his chronometer in his hand counting – I'm sure it was a chronometer, for I'd handled many a one in my time – and then I got my bashing.

The first stroke went right across my shoulders, and it was something awful. I'd never felt anything like it before, and I howled out sharp, and roared as loud as I could. Just where the lash went it seemed to burn right into me, and the skin felt as if it had swelled up and was going to burst. It went through me like, and if a hot iron had scorched me it wouldn't have been half as sharp.

I'd been told by the old 'uns in the gaol that it was best to shout, as the doctor would think it was hurting me bad, and I might get off with half the dose, and I kept on all the time it lasted. I could have said to the doctor, 'You _____ pig' as quiet as I'm saying it to you now, for crying didn't ease me a bit. It was only a bit of kidment to 'scheme' the doctor but it didn't work.

It was slow time, for I counted thirty before I got number two, and that came as sharp as the first. I cursed and called them every _____ thing I could get off my tongue, for I felt savage at being shoved in for what I didn't deserve.

The doctor stood close by, and pointed out where every stroke was to drop, and the screw put

it down just where he shewed. He was a bad 'un that doctor, for every cut was as bad as the others, and the pain was just like dying over and over again. What did I think about between the lashes? I don't know, for I was cursing as hard as I could. You see, I did think I'd done many things that I ought to have got a lashing for, but now I was innocent. I couldn't help that coming into my head during the half minute between the lashes, but the hardest pull was trying to make out where the next would drop. The doctor would point, and I waited till I heard the whip coming, and then I cried out, louder every time. Sometimes it would drop on one of the cuts that had gone before, and it was _____ bad then.

I could have sworn my back was as big again as it should be, for after the cat was pulled sharp back the flesh went after it, and rose up till I knew I was bleeding, and that the skin had burst. The blood ran down into my trousers thick, no cheese [mistake] about it. How did it hurt me? Why, every now and then the cat lapped round my chest, and that was worst of all. It knocked me out of wind, my breath went as if I'd jumped into cold water, choking like, and my mouth as dry as could be. I'd nothing to chew, so I hung on to the rings with my hands as hard as I could, and this only pulled my chest across the wood and made my back tighter. I bled a good deal but I got the two dozen, and I felt every odd 'un. The last was as bad as the first, every bit of it, if not a trifle smarter, but I shouldn't have minded if they'd laid it on quicker. It was the slow time that licked me, and if I'd had the regulation three dozen I think it would have done for me. It's all stupid about not feeling it after the first five or six. Your back don't grow dead at all, but only gets tender as you get more of it.

Is there anything else like a bashing? Nothing that I know of. I've had most kinds of knocking about, but it licks all; there's no punishment comes anywhere near it. It's as bad while you're waiting as when you're getting it, and both are smart. When I was taken down I was properly done over, and my back was bleeding in a dozen places. I was swelled all round too, in a way you couldn't believe, and I couldn't button my trousers or put my braces on, although before I was scrat I could have wrapped my trouser's band half a dozen inches over. They were prison clothes and they throw them at you, and ain't particular about the fit. I was sore for a good many days, but I wouldn't go to hospital or see the doctor. I knew I'd to go through the mill, and I meant to do every bit of it without flinching. I gave my head to it, and when one of the screws came round and asked me if my back had done bleeding I told him I was all right. I went to chapel the day

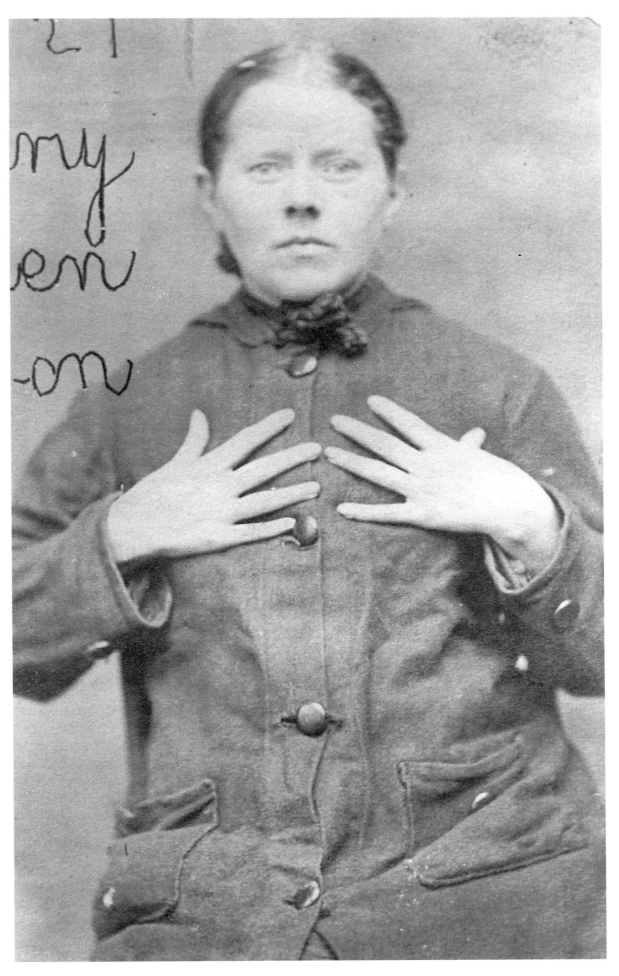

63. Mary Ellen Wilson. A rare example of a female burglar who served eight months for robbing the Gowan hotel in 1881.

I shall never forget the morning I was brought out to be flogged, which happened about a week after I went in. When I got into the great yard I saw the governor, the surgeon, the chaplain and about forty prisoners, the latter with their faces towards the wall.

When the triangle was brought out I began to shake from head to foot. It appeared that several had to be flogged; and to make matters more unpleasant, so far as I was concerned, a number had to undergo the punishment before me.

When the first was strapped he began to shout and roar like a child, but the lash was nevertheless, administered with great force. Such crying or groaning I never heard before or since, and I hope I may never hear again. Amongst the rest were the following ejaculations:

'Do have pity!'

'Lord, save me!'

'Mercy! Mercy! you'll kill me!'

My name was called out at last, and I in turn began to cry for mercy and pardon; but it was only like the prophet of Baal calling unto their god – no help came. On the contrary, the more I cried for mercy the more severely was the lash felt. At length I was released from the triangle, and marched slowly to my cell. On arriving there I fell down from exhaustion, and was scarcely able to lie in bed for pain.

BRITAIN'S MOST WANTED MAN

John Jackson, like many professional thieves, was something of a specialist. Whilst others stole from shops, houses and factories, the 33-year-old painter and plumber targeted the Salvation Army. Knowing the hours when members were beating tambourines and singing the hallelujah chorus, he broke into headquarters to steal money destined for the poor.

Jackson's lack of imagination was to become his undoing. In 1888, following a spate of robberies from missions, the police staked out the Salvation Army hostel in Eccles. Jackson was captured leaving the premises with his booty: a signature stamp, a money-box and 2d. He was sentenced to six months in Strangeways.

Following the customary one month in solitary confinement, Jackson was assigned various jobs about the prison. A gas leak had been reported in the matron's quarters, and, under the supervision of Ralph Webb, the burly 45-year-old warder, Jackson set about the minor repairs. Having once previously escaped from prison, and with the bulk of his sentence before him, the prisoner, working so near the wall and armed with a set of tools, could not let the opportunity pass.

64. Jane Grey alias Jane Gaylor, also known as 'Hoppy's woman'. Hoppy was Eliah Gaylor, an old con who had been transported and returned to his mother country. He was described as a clever cockney. Jane was sentenced to nine months in March 1874 but died in the city gaol after serving just six months.

after the bashing, for I wouldn't give in though needn't have gone unless I'd liked.

I stayed in gaol 13 weeks and was then sent to the Bank [Millbank Prison]. My back was healed then but the marks were there, and when I got in the bath with the others, they made some remarks about it, but I didn't care. There were a dozen of us from Manchester, and we were such thin, poor-looking devils the doctor said we must be badly off in this part of the country.

SECOND FLOGGING IN MANCHESTER

Henry Holloway was also sentenced to a taste of the cat in Manchester gaol. He described the dehumanising ordeal in *'An Echo From Prison '* published in 1877.

THE MURDER IN THE MATRONS BED ROOM

65. After attacking the warder, Jackson stole his boots and escaped through a hole in the ceiling.

Hearing strange sounds overhead where the repairs were being effected, the matron, Miss Little, went to check that all was in order. It most certainly was not. Lying on the floor and bleeding profusely from a single wound to the back of the head was the warder. There was no sign of the prisoner but a hole hurriedly knocked through the roof left no doubt that the bird had flown. Jackson had stolen Webb's boots and jumped 10ft. to the streets below. The weapon, a hammer, was later recovered from the roof. Despite the brutal force of the blow, which severely fractured the base of his skull, Webb was still conscious, though in deep shock. He kept asking what had happened to his boots. Webb didn't need them where he was going. He succumbed to his injuries a short time later.

Jackson already had a reputation as a rogue and bully, but his cold-blooded, cowardly assault on warder Webb caused him to become, in the first half of 1888, the country's most wanted man. A dangerous and cunning murderer was on the loose and his exploits were followed avidly in the press. He was the front-page story on the *Illustrated Police News* for three consecutive weeks. Manchester's top detective, Jerome Caminada, was assigned to the case.

On the night of the escape, Saturday May 22, 1888, two burglaries were committed in Oldham. In the first clothes were stolen and prison issue left behind. The thief, an experienced pro, nonchalantly smoked stolen cigars as he took his time selecting his new garb. The second break-in left police in no doubt as to the perpetrator. The victim was a captain in the Salvation Army. The educated murderer appeared to be enjoying himself, even leaving a note behind, quoting Shakespeare, 'Good bye Captain – though lost to sight, to memory dear."

On the reverse side he thoughtfully listed the amount stolen: £1.16s.

Jackson kept moving, covering his tracks in Halifax, Leeds and Bradford.

66. Webb was still alive when discovered but died a short time later.

In the wake of the widespread publicity pursuing him, however, some locals soon became suspicious of strangers. Despite his changed appearance, Jackson was recognised by a mason, who'd offered him lodgings. Marshall Booth, the man responsible for Jackson's capture, told his story to the police:

The prisoner has been staying a week in Bradford. He spent all his time in public houses and has been regarded by all who came in contact with him as a jolly good fellow. The prisoner evidently enjoyed good company, and sang songs which evoked considerable praise. Some of the men with whom he associated felt a curiosity as to his antecedents, and asked him where he came from, to which he replied, "From Garnett street in Bradford". Suspicion, however arose and on Sunday night I refused to let him sleep with me, although he had been sleeping in the house for several days. The prisoner, nevertheless, came to the house again late at night and tried to gain admission. I said to a friend:

"There's something queer about this man. I'm afraid he's Jackson. Let's go and collar him."

We then ran after Jackson and overtook him, and we tackled him. A policeman was sent for, and eventually Jackson was overpowered and handcuffed. He remarked as he held up his hands for the handcuffs: "I'm done," and gave in without the least show of further resistance.

In the course of the official struggle both Booth and the prisoner were bruised, particularly the latter, who had a wound on his head caused by a kick.

It appeared that Jackson had received a good 'going-over'.

At the police-station Detective Inspector Dobson and Detective Talbot were assigned the task of determining the identity of the prisoner, who would only answer to the name of Thomas Harrison. Dobson takes up the story:

Talbot took him over to the cells along with the printed description issued, and after stripping him, compared him mark for mark, and found them all to correspond. He then said it's no use you denying it, you are Firth [Jackson was one of several aliases] and the prisoner replied, 'I am.' They came back to me then, and I said to the prisoner. 'Do you really say you are Jackson?' and he again replied 'I am.' After this to make sure, I took him back myself and examined him thoroughly, and found every mark as described, the scar on the thigh, the mole on the left side, the scar on his eye, and the lump on the inside of the hand. I was sure by this time that he was the man.

PORTRAIT OF JACKSON SKETCHED IN COURT.

67. Jackson specialised in breaking into Salvation Army premises. He stole clothes and £1.16s. in Oldham, and, after smoking a cigar, left a receipt!

Jackson's clothes matched those listed as being stolen and he was brought before the Bradford police court and handed over to Manchester police to face the charge of murdering assistant warder Webb.

A large crowd assembled at the train station, all trying to catch a glimpse of Britain's most wanted man. The authorities were determined he would not evade them a second time and Jackson was transported to the county police court in a van with a large police escort.

His trial a month later attracted many ladies dressed in the height of fashion. Jackson, in contrast, appeared in an old rusty black suit and had grown a beard and moustache. He looked pale and weak and, as was the norm, pled 'not guilty'. He took a lively interest in the proceedings.

The defence case was very weak but, several decades before the argument became fashionable, Jackson's counsel protested that his client could not have a fair trial as the popular press had already found him guilty! He went on to submit an explanation of the events of 21st May so outrageous it would have been laughable had it not involved the death of a human being. Mr. Wharton (defence counsel) argued that Webb (the warder) tripped over the carpet just as his client was swinging back his hammer in the course of the repairs.

Mr. Justice Grantham, in his summing up, made short shrift of the accident theory, arguing that it

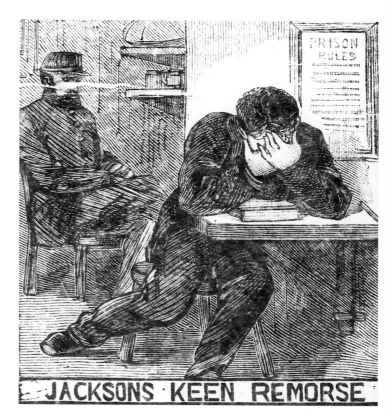

JACKSONS KEEN REMORSE

69. The scourge of the Salvation Army was hanged some eleven weeks after the murder of the warder.

was a monstrous improbability. The jury agreed and returned a verdict of 'guilty' within seven minutes.

Jackson's last words in court were:

"I never intended to strike him."

He was hanged on 7th August 1888 and his body interred in the prison yard. Jackson, once Britain's most wanted man, was quickly forgotten to be replaced in that role, that very month, by Whitechapel's notorious slayer of prostitutes.

RELEASE FROM STRANGEWAYS

George Harrison thanked his sweet lord when his day of release from a 6 month spell in Strangeways finally arrived. He vividly recalls his last few hours in an article for the *Manchester Evening News* in 1905:

At last I get up, and having had much practice I roll up my bedclothes in the regulation manner in the dark, wash myself, and wait. Whilst doing so I fix up my sheets, pillowslip, towel, brush and comb, prayer-book and Bible, ready to take to the entrance hall with me. These are treated as a prisoner's personal property whilst he is in prison, given to him on entering and returned by him on leaving…

Most of the poor beggars have only to put out their water cans &c., and close their doors again, but there are three beside myself who are going to their anxious friends, and who are promptly lined up. But although we are only an hour or two from

JACKSON FULLY COMMITTED

68. Jackson's last words in court were: *"I never intended to strike him."*

70. Crowds gathering outside Strangeways to read the official notification of an execution. Of the 44 hanged at Strangeways to 1914, 42 were male.

freedom, discipline must be preserved, so we have to go down two flights of stairs with as nearly as possible four yards between man and man. We are then lined up on the ground floor with many others wearing khaki. There are almost as many wearing the official blue, who are there, I suppose, to see that the outgoing prisoners don't break gaol.

Suddenly I hear a call "Harrison! Any of you called George Harrison?" I own up and am handed a letter saying that as it is now January, and I was fool enough to be captured in Summer, I may be pleased to know that my overcoat will be waiting for me at the gates. I am! I ought to have had the letter before, but had received my full compliment – four in six months (including a tailor's bill).

The roll is now called. There are eighty-four of us outward bound, and we march off in very open order to the dressing rooms. We have left all our prison belongings where we have been standing, so are marching light. We discard our coats and vests in the first room, and are then ushered into a large flagged room walled with dressing boxes, which the builder has forgotten to supply with doors. We have to strip which we could have done in the centre of the floor without any more severe shock to our modesty. But everyone is in the same boat, so no one laughs at anyone else.

At last we get our own clothes, and although they have been fumigated since we saw them, I, for one, feel altogether different after getting them on, and somehow my feet feel comfortable in boots, for the first time in six months.

One more step forward, and now we are allowed to talk to our fellow man, but it must be quietly. This is in the breakfast saloon, where there are trays of gruel and bread on the floor. Many poor chaps, who don't know where to get their next meal, devour a double portion, and then put a cob or two in their pockets. But there are others who have ham and eggs waiting outside, so the stock lasts.

Now we pass one by one through the chief warder's office, and receive the cash the police have kindly left us. Then another long rest during which one of our number is sent back to his cell until evening for laughing with joy. Another roll call and a funeral march to the gates. Once more our names are called over, and slowly we emerge to the lambient atmosphere of Southall-street.

The year George Harrison left Strangeways saw a change to the usual inhabitant, political prisoners joined the ranks of murderers and ne'er-do-wells.

A journalist from the *Manchester Evening Chronicle* was sent to Strangeways on October 20th, 1905. This is his report:

71. With the new century Strangeways was forced to house a new type of prisoner.

72. The arrest outside the University may have been a student protest or related to the Suffragette movement. Protesters would often refuse to pay fines and spend a few days inside to gain publicity for their cause.

EXIT THE HEROINE

At five minutes past seven the ponderous gates were opened, and slowly there emerged in the half light a procession of fallen sisters, with their shawls drawn tightly over their heads, one hugging a baby. As they were eyed by the waiting crowd the coverings were drawn closer round their pale pinched faces, and they slunk out of sight as quickly as their legs would carry them, no doubt glad enough to be free.

In another minute the people's patience had its reward when Miss Christabel, with light step and smiling face, appeared from the gloomy portals. She was hailed with a great cheer and instantly surrounded by a host of male and female admirers, who must have embarrassed the maid by their greeting.

First to greet and embrace the fair prisoner was her mother, Mrs. Pankhurst. It was an affecting scene. Miss Pankhurst fell into the arms of her mother, and the two wept with joy after having been parted for a whole week. The ex-prisoner's friends then closed round her, and presented her with beautiful bunches of chrysanthemums and lilies of the valley. As soon as she could break away from her admirers Miss Pankhurst called out, "I will go in again for the same cause. Don't forget the vote for women." Mrs. Pankhurst asked the people not to forget the principle for which her daughter had suffered. They must press forward and never rest, especially the women, until the vote had been secured.

The party then boarded a cab and drove away amidst the cheers of the crowd.

The suffragette movement drew together women of disparate backgrounds, who would probably never have met but for their common sense of injustice. On Friday 13th October 1905, Christabel Pankhurst, an outstanding law student at Owens College, and Annie Kenney, a cotton mill worker, determined to put the controversial topic of votes for women on the agenda of a Liberal meeting to be held at the Free Trade Hall.

Two alleged supporters of the movement, Sir Edward Grey and the young Winston Churchill (candidate for North-West Manchester) addressed the audience in search of votes for the coming election. Women were expected to remain silent (and make the sandwiches?) at such gatherings, but nothing could have been further from the intentions of the two young militants.

Annie was the first to break the unwritten rule. Rising from her seat she came straight to the point.

"Will the Liberal Government give votes to women?"

There was no reply, the audience were stunned. Christabel leapt to her feet and the two young women unfurled their banner with its simple message.

'VOTES FOR WOMEN'

The mainly male audience began to find their voices. Stewards forced the protesters to sit down to a chorus of catcalls, jeers and sneers. The two women were placated for the time being by the promise of the Chief Constable that the question would be answered at the end of the meeting. It was simply ignored. Action of a more militant nature would be needed if the issue was to gain the attention of the newspapers. Determined to be heard, Christabel jumped onto a seat demanding an answer to her question. Both women were seized and dragged from the building. Christabel spat in the faces of the policemen, an act often employed by prostitutes, rarely by law students. Dumped in the street the two women determined to hold their own meeting and addressed the sizable crowd, many of whom had followed from the auditorium.

Arrested and charged with obstruction, both women appeared in court the following morning. Christabel was ordered to pay a fine of a half-guinea for assaulting the police and five shillings for obstruction. The alternative was seven days imprisonment. Annie was fined five shillings or three days. Both women refused all offers of help with the fines and opted for the cells. Let's hear what they made of their stay in Strangeways. Firstly Annie Kenney:

I remember very little of my life in prison. Being my first visit to gaol, the newness of the life numbed me. I do remember the plank bed, the skilly, the prison clothes. I also remember going to church and sitting next to Christabel, who looked very coy and pretty in her prison cap. She took my hand tenderly and just held it, as though I were a lost child being guided home. She guessed my feelings of strangeness, and no doubt I looked lonely and troubled.

I scarcely ate anything all the time I was in prison, and Christabel told me later that she was glad when she saw the back of me, it worried her to see me looking pale and vacant.

Christabel looked upon her stay behind bars as unpleasant but necessary if the movement was to gain publicity and support:

I have been doing the ordinary prison work, serving, scrubbing and cell-cleaning, but mind you say that I don't complain in the least.

With Christabel's university threatening to expel her if a similar incident occurred, she kept a lower profile thereafter as the fight moved on to London.

MANCHESTER'S SHERLOCK HOLMES

73. Jerome Caminada used to meet his informers in the back pews of the hidden gem church. (St. Mary's).

The man responsible for putting so many of the inmates of Strangeways behind bars was the super sleuth Jerome Caminada who personally knew all the back-alleys of Manchester and most of the villains who lived in them.

Manchester's most famous detective, Jerome Caminada, a Catholic of Italian and Irish extraction, was a policeman on a mission to clean up the city's streets. Nothing escaped Jerome's attention and he would show as much enthusiasm for tracking down coal merchants who made short deliveries, as he did hunting dangerous murderers. Once a case was brought to his attention he doggedly saw it through to its conclusion, bringing all manner of criminals, from petty-thieves to murderers, to book.

For those interested in Caminada's life and cases I would recommend the two volumes *Twenty-five years of Detective life* (1895). The first volume has recently been reprinted and some of the chapter titles reveal the breadth of his interests:

How I punished a wife-beater.

Next of kin frauds.

Manchester anarchists at work.

Street pests.

Just a few stories give the flavour and nature of crimes of the times.

74. A selection of police accessories employed in Victorian Manchester.

SWEATY PALMS

As early as the 1870s there was a very lucrative living to be made in medicine. Doctors could charge sick patients very high fees for consultations and prescriptions knowing they would pay almost any amount to relieve their pain. Tempted by the prospects of easy money, several quacks set up shop in Manchester. They would spend a great deal of money advertising, mostly with handbills, requesting patients to seek consultation in their 'surgeries'. These were usually hired rooms, impressively decked out with hundreds of bottles of multi-coloured medicines and heavy volumes of medical books. Some of these fraudsters deliberately tried to frighten their patients following the latters' production of the obligatory urine sample. They did this by secretly placing a small portion of the white of an egg into a test-tube. When the urine was added and heated over a lighted spirit-lamp, the albumen would boil and float to the top of the liquid. The doctors would then tell their terrified patients the egg was semen *'which would inevitably cause consumption .'* There was a cure but it would cost several pounds. The thankful patient left, desperately clutching a bottle of medicine, minus the equivalent of about one month's salary.

Caminada determined to tackle the problem personally, and, equipped with bogus symptoms, presented himself as a warehouseman to several physicians. His aim was to eventually prosecute them for the fraudulent use of title M.D. Most of the detective's visits followed a similar path to that related below:

On the night of 13th October I went to the defendant's place of business in Grosvenor Street. I told defendant I had a pain in my heart, and was troubled with sweating hands. He asked me had I ever been guilty of self-pollution. I said 'No, never.' He then reached a pint tumbler from the table, and asked me to make water in it. I said nothing ailed my water, and he replied 'I can tell if anything is the matter with you from that'. I refused to comply with his request.

After considering a short time defendant said 'Have you £3 and I will give you a case of medicine which will put you right in five or six weeks?' (Laughter). I said 'No I will give you 10s each time I come, once a week for six weeks.' He replied 'No, I must have it all at once; but have you got a sovereign?' I said I had a sovereign, and for that he offered to make me up a bottle of medicine. He gave me the bottle produced, for which I gave him 20s. I said 'Give me a book or a bill on nervousness.'

He said 'The best thing is to get cured – you want no book.' I said 'Give me one for the sovereign'. He replied 'If you get a book, it will drive you mad. You want some good medicine'. I asked him for a receipt for the money. He became angry, and said 'What the devil is it you do want? I cannot give bills.' He put his hand into his pocket, and taking out a sovereign said 'If you like I will take back my medicine.' I said 'No I would rather keep it at present.' (Laughter). He afterwards said 'I will give you a bill when I have cured you. I do not like taking a case in hand without making a cure.' He advised me to take a wine glass of the medicine every morning and to see him when it was done.

Mr. Estcourt said the medicine given to Detective Caminada was a compound decoction of sarsaparilla. Mr. Lund stated that this preparation would increase the perspiration of a man troubled with sweating hands! Defendant was fined £5 with costs.

When telling another 'doctor' about the pain in his heart and sweaty palms Caminada was again questioned as to whether he had been guilty of *self-pollution* (the solitary vice). The defendant, in this case one Benjamin Key, like many criminals in the Manchester area, wanted to grab hold of Caminada by the testicles. The detective refused insisting:

"I am all right there."

Key was adamant: "I must examine them, because if they are hanging down, you want some bracing medicine to clip them up."

Caminada once again refused: "It is not for that I want to be treated: it is for sweating hands."

Furnished with these same ailments, Caminada visited numerous other quacks, some of whom prescribed the following treatments, all of course for a substantial fee: Caminada was told to turn on the water-tap every morning, swill his head and shoulders and rub them with a towel; he was forbidden to drink green tea; told to go to theatres and concerts and ride outside omnibuses.

The medicines prescribed were analysed and found to contain, amongst others, the following ingredients: rhubarb magnesia; spirits of lavender; compound camphor; perchlorate of iron; sarsaparilla and water flavoured with chinchona bark.

All the defendants were found guilty and given a range of fines up to £20.

DISGRACEFUL PROCEEDINGS IN MANCHESTER – MEN DRESSED IN FEMALE ATTIRE.

Thus ran the headline in the *Illustrated Police News* of October 9th. 1880. Following a tip off, the police, under the supervision of Detective Sergeant Caminada, were discreetly keeping surveillance on a temperance hall hired for a ball, off York Street. To do the story justice, here are some extracts from the original report, composed in a shocked, puritanical style:

About nine o'clock cabs began to arrive at the hall, the occupants being young men, who in most instances brought either portmanteaus or tin boxes with them. A considerable number were in female attire, the characters of historical and other personages being assumed. The apparel of the persons who appeared as women was of an elaborate description, and among the costumes were several low-bodied dresses, "Juliet" being conspicuous among the grotesque assumptions. Bracelets and jewellery of a tawdry description were worn and the

75. Caminada watched the proceedings from behind a chimney stack. The dances were described as 'grotesque, such as are familiar at low-class music halls'.

RAID UPON A FANCY

76. Cross-dressing was considered the height of depravity (well, publicly at least!)

common glittering adjuncts in such dresses were to be seen. Among the personages represented by persons in male attire were Henry V111., Richard 111., Sir Walter Raleigh, Romeo and naval officers. In all forty-seven persons entered the building and of these twenty-two were dressed as women.

Dancing commenced about ten o'clock, the orchestra consisting of a harmonium, at which a blind man named Mark Letcher, of Manchester, presided. All but two of the windows had been screened, so that no one outside the hall could see what was going on; but the two which had been left open for ventilation enabled the police to see all that transpired in the ball-room.

Detective Caminada ascended the roof of an

adjacent building, from which he could obtain a view of the proceedings in the hall, and remained there for a considerable time, concealing himself from observation behind a chimney stack. The company engaged chiefly in grotesque dances, such as are familiar at low-class music-halls. Shortly before one o'clock in the morning, Caminada having satisfied himself of the impropriety of the proceedings, made arrangements for a raid upon the company...

More than a dozen constables were called to the spot by signal when all was ready, and they were drawn up in file alongside the building without their movements being heard. Caminada then knocked gently at the door, but received no answer. He

DRESS BALL

knocked in all seven times and then some person inside said "Who's there?" The officer had learned that the password being adopted was "sister" and imitating a female voice, he gave the word.

The door was at once opened and the police rushed into the building. Several of the dancers attacked the police, with the object of forcibly ejecting them, and Caminada was hurled back into the doorway. Quickly recovering himself he seized two men who were nearest to him, and in a few moments every person present was in custody. Some of them succeeded in throwing off portions of the female dresses which they had assumed, and others were in the act of doing so when they were seized…

The police were assisted by a number of working men whom Caminada had called upon, and after being handcuffed the prisoners were taken in batches to the Park place and Knot Mill Police stations, and subsequently to the Town Hall, where they were lodged in the cells connected with the detective department. Several cab-loads of apparel were brought away and lodged at the Town-Hall…

In court the scene was a remarkable one, all the prisoners appearing in the attire in which they were arrested. Detective Sergeant Caminada described the arrest and the manner in which the defendants were secured by the handcuffs in order to restrain them from violence. On applying for a remand, the chairman said:

"What is the particular offence they are charged with?"

Detective Caminada: "There was a sort of dance to very quick time, which my experience has taught me is the "can-can". The men in female attire took a prominent part in the dance. The officer then went on to describe what he saw took place, mentioning that the men dressed as women were so well disguised that at first he failed to recognise them. There was not a single woman there and the proceedings were too coarse to describe. He made that observation because, in society, there existed a class of men, almost unknown to many gentlemen, who prowl about the streets almost to the same extent as unfortunate women, and some of the prisoners belonged to that class…

The prisoners were then remanded to Thursday. They left the court as quickly as possible, and several of them raised their garments to conceal their faces from the spectators in the gallery…

The prisoners were conveyed from the police cells at the Town Hall to the court in Minshull-street in cabs. Eight of them were in female ball apparel, and several of their companions were attired as historic notabilities. As they filed into the dock… the spectators could not suppress an outburst of laughter. The prisoners seemed to be considerably ashamed of their position, some of them screening their faces with their arms and hats as they entered and left the court.

There was a remand period of a few days so the prosecution could fully prepare its case.

On Thursday morning the prisoners were brought up on remand at the Manchester City Police-court. The court was crowded, and many hundreds of people were unable to gain admission. The prisoners were in their ordinary dresses, and many of them appeared to feel deeply their position. The prisoners were charged with meeting together for the purpose of inciting one another to commit abominable offences. Their offence was one which was unnameable. The punishment for this offence was fixed – for the offence itself not more than ten years' penal servitude, and not less than three years' for the misdemeanour of inciting persons to commit this offence…

On the conclusion of the case for the prosecution, counsel for the defendants urged that no case of such serious nature as to warrant commitment had been established. The justices after consultation, decided to bind the defendants over in two sureties of £25 each, to be of good behaviour for twelve months, or in default be imprisoned for three months.

FAR FROM ELEMENTARY

Just over a year after Sherlock Holmes was first introduced to the public in *A Study in Scarlet*, Manchester's real-life answer to the fictional detective wrapped up what was probably his most famous case, the Manchester Cab Murder. In just three weeks a murder suspect was detected, a case presented and a verdict of guilty returned, though the case was far from elementary, for two reasons.

Firstly it had to be determined whether a murder had indeed been committed. Secondly, if it had, the sole lead was a vague description of a young man, 5' 3", similar to thousands who regularly clubbed and pubbed in central Manchester.

At approximately 7 p.m. on Tuesday 26th February 1889, two mismatched drinking companions hailed a growler (a four-wheeled horse-drawn cab – not it's driver) near the Cathedral. The age difference between the two men was such that they could have been mistaken as an elderly father and his young son. Both had obviously been freely imbibing so it came as no surprise to Henry Goulding, the cabbie, when he was directed to another watering hole – the Three Arrows Tavern in Deansgate. Henry was told to hold his horse as the two men supped their bitter and slumped into the carriage again fifteen minutes later. The new destination was a house in Stretford Road, Hulme. Nearing the address Henry heard the cry all cabbies dreaded. A pedestrian shouted to him that his cab door was open and a young man was sprinting away. Reining in his horse, Henry let forth a torrent of oaths. Runners, or their Victorian equivalent, were the bane of his life. Resignedly he looked into his cab to find the older man slumped in the seat, barely conscious. Such was the cabby's lot – one runner and one inebriate. Henry, determined to get his fare, shook the man in the cab:

"Go away and leave me alone" were the last words uttered by the inebriate. He promptly slumped into the corner with a sigh, whereupon all signs of life disappeared. There were no indications that a struggle had taken place. It simply appeared that the session had been too much for the older man, who had succumbed to the demon drink. Henry was having a bad day but not nearly as bad as that of John Fletcher, the corpse in the cab.

John, a widower, was a rich businessman who had made his fortune in paper. He was an obvious target for any would-be thief or pickpocket, openly flaunting his wealth in the form of a gold pocket watch worth £120 – considerably more than a year's income for many workers. John's weakness was that he liked a tipple, and once on a bender seemed to show little concern for his own well-being. When searched at the infirmary, the watch, a chamois purse containing gold sovereigns and a pair of gold-rimmed glasses were missing.

There appeared an open and shut case of theft against the young runner but whether he would have to face a capital charge depended on the coroner's report, and of course, whether the police could find him.

Jerome Caminada was assigned to the case. Well known amongst the criminal underworld and indeed respected by some, Caminada would occasionally meet his snouts in the back pews of the hidden gem, the Church of St. Mary's. In order to obtain a lead on the younger man, who was the chief suspect, the detective needed to build up a picture of the deceased man's movements. Caminada put the word out. Information soon began to trickle in.

Fletcher – the deceased – had been seen with a younger man at an oyster stall. The landlady of the Three Arrows remembered serving beer to the two men, the elder settling the bill. It was in the York Minster, High Chatham, near where the man had jumped from the cab, that Caminada got his first good lead.

A man flush with gold sovereigns and sporting an extremely expensive watch could not help but be noticed and remembered. On the night of Fletcher's death, just such a man had stopped long enough to down a beer and have a cab sent for. Caminada was on the trail. The cabman was swiftly traced and remembered taking his fare to the Locomotive Inn, Oldham Road, New Cross – a place known to locals as 'Jack Rooks', a notorious haunt for young pugilists.

Why, Caminada asked himself, would anybody want to frequent such a pub? For the same reason we all do, was the answer: he wanted to mix with people having similar interests to himself. The thief, Caminada concluded, was probably a practitioner of the noble art. A motley crew with flat noses and cauliflower ears were duly interviewed and asked if they knew anything about the crime. One name kept cropping up – *Pig Jack* or more exactly, *Pig Jack's' son*.

77. An excellent photo of horse-drawn transportation. Perhaps 'Henry the Growler' is looking for fares. Where are all the female population?

Pig was not the sort of man to poke fun at. He was more than capable of looking after himself and therefore well-qualified to run a beerhouse in Greengate, Salford. His beer certainly seemed to have some special kick in it, for any regulars thrown out could inevitably manage only two or three steps before collapsing onto the pavement. They would wake up the next morning minus their cash, which in any case, they'd probably stolen.

It wasn't just the beer, however, that caused them to lose consciousness. Quite fittingly for an ex-boxer, Pig would covertly beef up the bevvies of apparently flush customers with knock-out drops.

Once adept at the druggists' art, Pig determined to play for higher stakes. With his main interest being boxing, the landlord was a regular at the bare-knuckle butchery that passed for prize fighting in pub basements. Large bets were struck on the outcome of each fight and there was easy money to be made if one knew the winner in advance. To influence matters, Pig knew just how much chloral to introduce into mouth rinses used between rounds. Passing the spiked mouthwash to one boxer, he would simply bet upon the other.

When discovered Pig knew he faced a worse punishment from his fellow pugilists than any the police could mete out. He took their advice and got out of town. Pig, however, had taught his son how to box, and, maybe, Caminada reasoned, he had also passed on his pharmaceutical knowledge.

When questioned about the John Fletcher affair, the 18-year-old Charles Parton denied all knowledge of it, stating that he was in Liverpool on the relevant night. At this stage, there was still no proof that Fletcher had been murdered.

When two gold sovereigns were discovered beneath his bed, Charles Parton was arrested and identified by several people as the man they had seen drinking with Fletcher on the night he died. Henry the Growler also picked him out, having doubtless made a mental note to tap him for the fare later.

Even first-rate detectives need a little luck. When sifting through some paperwork, Caminada's attention was drawn to a routine police report relating to a theft from a chemist's shop in Liverpool. On February 19th, a young man had attempted to purchase 40 grains of chloral – a hypnotic and anaesthetic hydrate. The chemist agreed to supply only ten grains, but as he was painstakingly measuring it out, the young man had reached over and snatched the bottle, fleeing the scene as quickly as he had subsequently fled the growler. The chemist later identified Parton.

Caminada was now certain he knew the cause of Fletcher's death: Parton had introduced chloral into Fletcher's beer in order to drug and eventually rob him.

Now that the medical men knew what they were looking for, traces of chloroform (decomposed chloral hydrate) were found in the internal organs of the victim.

When details of the crime were reported in the press two more victims came forward. Both had been drugged and robbed by Parton.

After 20 minutes deliberation the jury returned a verdict of *'guilty of murder with a strong recommendation for mercy'*. Such recommendations were not always acted upon and the judge warned the teenager:

It is my solemn duty to tell you, you must be prepared to die – you have forfeited your life to the law. I beg you as earnestly as I can to repent of this crime – do not build upon the recommendation which the jury have added to their verdict...

Effectively Caminada's role was now over. He had, with a little luck and a great deal of intuition, obtained a conviction for a capital offence which could easily have passed unnoticed.

The story, though, was not yet over. We need now to focus on Charles Parton as he languished in the condemned cell in Kirkdale Prison. Let's hear from the man himself:

For breakfast I had 8 oz of bread and a pint of porridge, and the same in the evening, and usually bully beef, bad potatoes, and bread at midday. We had pudding and soup three times a week. That wouldn't have been so bad if there had been enough, but being a healthy lad I had a big appetite, and was almost starving with the meagre fare.

Most of all I longed for a cup of tea. One day an official from the Home Office called to ask if I had any last request. "Yes" I replied "give me a cup of tea!" After a lot of trouble and fuss my request was granted.

I broke down only once in the condemned cell. My mother and father, brothers and sister, came to say goodbye. The parting took place in a room divided into two by iron bars. I was on one side of the room, my loved ones on the other. In the middle was a passage-way with iron bars on both sides, and up and down this a warder walked to make sure we did not try to shake hands. Two other warders were there to make sure no signs were passed.

78. *Charles Parton and John Fletcher set out on a city centre pub crawl.*

I was not even allowed a farewell kiss from my mother. All I could do was to stand in my blue prison clothes and read the pain and misery in the eyes of my dear ones. When the interview, which lasted only a few minutes, was over and I was led away, my tiny sister called out, "This way, Charlie," and pointed to the door they had come in by. She thought I was at liberty to go with them, not knowing my life was forfeit.

The warders who watched over me night and day in the condemned cell tried to cheer me up as best they could, but what alleviation could there be from the thought ever in my mind that each day brought me nearer the scaffold?

Time seemed to move incredibly swiftly. The day fixed for my death was about three weeks from the date of sentence. They still kept me on the fourth-class diet allowed under prison regulations. This was to me, a strong healthy youth of eighteen, practically starvation rations. I was hungry all the time.

The fourth day from the date fixed for my execution I was sitting talking to the warder on guard when the Chief Warder appeared. In his hand he held a sheet of official looking paper.

"Well, Parton," he said, "they've let you off."

After eleven years hard labour in Portland and Dartmoor prisons, Parton became the first man ever to be released in under twelve years. His mother mounted a campaign and enlisted the help of medical experts. One argued that the amount of chloral introduced into the drink – 30 grains, would not even have killed a baby. He argued that John Fletcher would in all probability have died that night from a heart condition, with or without the drug. Parton, however, was not pardoned but given a ticket-of-leave, which meant that if apprehended again he faced the prospect of serving out the rest of his sentence.

At 29, Parton set off to see the world he had dreamed about when breaking rocks over the previous eleven years. He worked his way through Canada, South Africa and New Zealand before settling in Argentina. It seems amazing that a man so wronged (as he thought) by his country, should voluntarily return to fight for it. But such was the case with Charles Parton, who returned to enlist to fight in the Great War.

He had not however, given up his thieving ways, and when apprehended for stealing a bag at Euston Station was sent down for six months. Once the authorities realised who they were housing in the cells they metaphorically threw away the keys. Parton was left to languish for almost four years before being freed at death's door. Without any certain date of release the ticket-of-leave man had lost the will to live and was only allowed out following medical advice.

The last news of Charles Parton saw him touring the country selling accounts of his life story.

THE EVIL THAT MEN DO...

CLEVER BURGLARS AND BULLIES

In the days before computerised data-bases, the police made copious notes of as many physical details as possible about offenders. This would aid future identification. Aliases were also noted. Manchester's police files included such characters as 'Paddy the Devil'; 'My Harry'; 'Collier Jack'; 'Cuddy Kit'; 'the Captain'; 'Cold Blow's Son'; 'Lucky Luke'; 'Jimmy the Greek'; 'Hoppy's woman' and 'Cranky Poll'. Surely the least original, however, were the aliases used by Leo McManus, a counterfeiter, who imaginatively used the aliases 'Smith' and 'Jones'.

Despite being copiously tattooed, paralysed in the right hand and foot and short of the tip of his third finger, John Monoghan lived in hope that he would not be recognised by the police. To avoid this catastrophe, he used a combination of deception and wishful thinking: six aliases and the hope no one would notice his limp. Neither ruse worked, he died with a record a mile long.

Other information kept by police on known offenders would certainly not pass any of today's criteria for political correctness. The entries under 'profession' were as bluntly honest as those listed were bent.

Amongst others, trades were entered as: clever burglar; clever travelling thief; travelling bank thief; thief and prostitute; labourer and bully; bully and thief; thief and clerk, and notorious dog thief and weaver.

Among the physical descriptions, phrases such as 'very bald' and 'very bad teeth' were in common usage, prior to being 'challenged' in recent years.

The following characteristics were noted in the prewar years:

Fond of women, well educated and well dressed.
Never wears a hat.
Quiet disposition, frowns.
Addicted to drink. Loose morals. Heavy cigarette smoker.
Weakness for stealing money.
Nervous disposition.
Fond of sport and company of women. Quick walker, usually carries pair of grey suede gloves and attache case. Wears snake-pattern watch chain.
Blinks his eyes when speaking.
Fond of racing. Walks erect.

Absolutely nothing was safe from thieves. Some rogues specialised in stealing from clothes lines, while others stole the lines themselves. Yet others were more inventive. Amongst goods noted as stolen around the turn of the century, in no special order, were: a hammer; a mallet; 28lbs of bones; three bottles of whiskey; a bag of rags; a copper ale warmer; a horse and trap; trousers; boots; beef; socks; a silver cream jug; an overcoat; five pigeons; two bells; potatoes; a rake; four petticoats and a set of false teeth.

When offenders succeeded in a particular type of crime, they would often seek to refine their skills throughout their criminal careers. It was by noting the modus operandi of law breakers in the Manchester area, that the police could find a likely list of suspects once details of new offences were circulated.

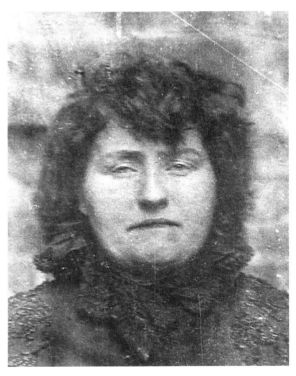

79. Alice Matthews, preyed on doctor's surgeries.

When thefts from doctor's surgeries were notified, Alice Matthews was the immediate prime suspect. She habitually sought medical assistance and if told that the G.P. was unavailable for some time, which often happened, would agree to wait before making off with anything that came to hand, her illness miraculously cured.

Harry Lancashire would pretend to be interested in public houses that came on the market. Posing as a prospective buyer he would visit the licensed premises and secrete about his body any booty that came to hand before telling the vendor that the pub did not quite fit the bill.

Another Harry, Mountford, had a passion for the railways and dressing up. His main hobby, however, was purloining other people's property. His heart beat must have been racing as, dressed in railwayman's uniform, he made off from the city's railway stations with stolen parcels.

A third Harry, Burke, was an expert letter-box thief. He inserted a piece of wire smeared with bird lime into a letter-box. The bird-lime would stick to the letter which he then removed and secreted.

Alfred Noakes would rifle churches in his search for the offertory box. There was no hiding place he could not unearth after breaking in. When it came to his chosen career, Alfred believed in the broad church, treating all denominations equally.

81. Ernest Schuler (alias Schiller). A German bully convicted in London and Manchester for living off the earnings of prostitutes.

80. Alfred Noakes specialised in breaking into churches and robbing offertory boxes.

Some thieves were Raffles-like characters, both very convincing and charming. John Connolly was a professional housebreaker, who used his powers of persuasion on respectable but gullible young ladies. He persuaded them to pawn his booty to unsuspecting pawnbrokers.

George Nevin was an accomplished shoplifter and hypocrite. He entered shops dressed as a clergyman and developed the habit of secreting goods about his religious garb. When challenged he would loudly proclaim his innocence and invariably tried to bluff his way out by threatening to call upon a minister to give evidence as to his good character.

One of the most plausible conmen, Thomas Pickford, would often pose as a solicitor's clerk from Canada, but his most successful role was that of detective. He chose his victims carefully – vulnerable women, owning or managing small shops. He would brashly enter their premises stating that he had a man in custody charged with

passing on forged notes. He would then ask to examine all the notes in the till, which were dutifully handed over. Following a cursory inspection Pickford would state that he needed to examine the banknotes at the police station and ask the owner

82. George Nevin, an expert shoplifter and hypocrite. He would pose as a man of the cloth to disguise his thieving ways.

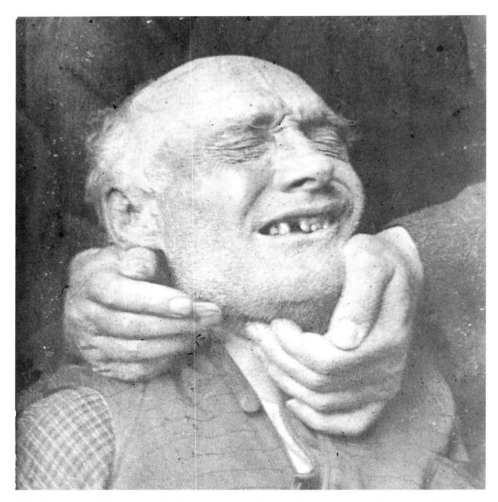

83. Thomas Murphy. A drunken waster with a string of convictions for offences such as refusing to pay cab fares, stealing purses etc. In the days before political correctness he was described in the police profile as being 'very bald with very bad teeth [i.e. follicly and dentally challenged !] aged 65 but looking younger.'

to accompany him. As they neared their destination the inspector made the excuse that he had another appointment, promising that he would join the shopkeeper at the station a few minutes later. The minutes of course turned to hours and the hours…

John William Marsland was the scourge of undertakers, whom he targeted for his con. He arrived in a distressed state at funeral parlours, where, shedding crocodile tears, he would claim that a relative had been killed in an accident some fair distance from Manchester. When the funeral director consented to undertake the burial, Marsland asked for a loan to make the longish journey to the scene of the accident, promising to send the funeral papers as soon as he arrived. They were left waiting along with the shopkeepers.

Arthur Edwards was in the market for second-hand clothes. Once a touch of frost got on the ground, keeping warm came second in the list of life's priorities, after keeping well nourished. Arthur would call upon the houses of relatives of men he knew to be working on building sites. He told whoever answered the knock, usually a wife, that

the man of the house had fallen into a lime pit full of water on the building site and was in need of a complete change of clothing, which he had been sent to convey to the site.

KNOWING A BITCH

Attitudes did not change with the death of little 'Vicky'. Homosexuality was considered one of the most heinous crimes and in the early years of the twentieth century two Manchester men were sentenced to ten years each for 'the abominable crime of buggery'. A young man 'carnally knowing' a girl over 13, but under 16, was sent down for nine months.

Thomas Taylor, a 16-year-old shoe repairer from Moss Side 'did feloniously, wickedly and against the order of nature carnally know a bitch'. Sensibly the judge refrained from giving him the cat and settled for six months gaol instead. Another animal lover of the same age was James Carlow, who was sent down for twelve months for committing the same offence with a cow and pony.

84. A relaxed-looking Catherine Read, alias Armstrong. The 27-year-old prostitute was charged with stealing clothes. Of more interest were the tattoos on her arms. What did they mean? Right arm: J A A N M A J N O D M A B. Left arm: M J W W K H N C M A J S J W.

86. Fredericia Parkins wanted to give her family a Christmas to remember. On 23rd. December she departed the butchers with two pheasants and a dead duck. Unfortunately she overlooked payment. Fredericia faced the holiday period behind bars if she couldn't find the 15s. fine.

85. Mary Wilson obviously took a pride in her appearance but harsh living conditions led to premature aging. Mary was 33 when the photo was taken.

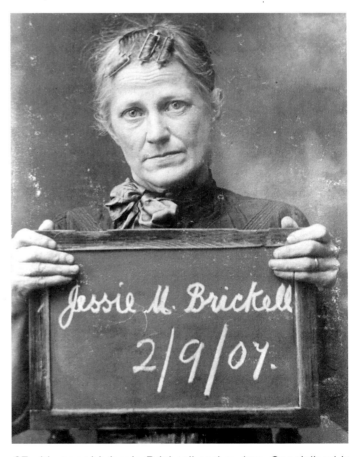

87. 44-year-old Jessie Bricknell and curlers. Specialised in stealing children's underclothes and shirts. Sentenced to 14 days H.L. in 1907.

88. Daniel '7 days' Davies. It was a hard life on the streets. Davies was sent down for 7 days for vagrancy, 7 days for begging and 7 days for sleeping out. One of the first victims of zero tolerance?

bound to maintain, now are actually charged to the Township of Manchester." It was another short sharp shock for our hero.

A FAIR COP

Detective-inspector Ashton kept a scrapbook of newspaper reports of cases in which he was involved. He served from 1883 to 1909 and certainly crossed swords with all manner of villains. William Ashton received no fewer than 105 awards from the Watch Committee. Here are examples of his various triumphs.

Female recalcitrants rarely came quietly. When under the influence of drink they would try to resist arrest and often spat in the arresting officer's face. A continual torrent of verbal abuse usually followed. Susy Williams, Mary Jane Allen and Elizabeth Jones, arrested for frequenting near the railway station, behaved in such a violent manner on the tram taking them to the police station that they had to be transferred to a cab. All three were sentenced to three months. In the dock Jones vowed to gain her revenge saying that she would 'have the life of Detective Ashton'.

Margaret Walker from Collyhurst Street had taken to the bottle in a big way. So much so that she neglected everything else in life including her children, who were found to be swarming with vermin. The home was in a most filthy condition and her husband could not trust her with any money, as this would invariably end up in the gin palace. She even pawned the children's things to satisfy her craving. When Ashton was sent to arrest her, Margaret Walker set about him in a frenzied attack, succeeding in biting him before being hauled to the station. She was sentenced to a drying out period of six months.

Those attempting to take their own lives or deprive their families of financial means, could also be dealt with in court. Jessie Stewart, a 30-year-old laundress with seven convictions for drunkenness and prostitution, was sentenced to fourteen days for attempting to take her own life. It was some decades before such behaviour was removed from the criminal lists.

James Tighe refused to contribute to his family's budget. Having already served 17 months as a result of 7 court appearances for the same offence, he once again appeared before the beak charged with being: "an incorrigible rogue, for that on 19th May 1903, being a person able to maintain himself and his family, by work and other means, hath wilfully refused and neglected to do so, whereby his wife and children, whom he is legally

Ashford never flinched from the dangerous job of Warrant officer. When sent to arrest George Thomas Farrell, the policeman knew, from his record, that he was unlikely to submit without a struggle.

The previous Saturday Farrell had tried hawking some ribs of bacon in the Bay Horse beerhouse on Rochdale road. Getting no takers, he sought to console himself with a bevvy or two. Farrell was well-known to the landlord, a Mr. Dawson, who refused to serve him because of previous offences committed whilst under the influence.

Farrell flipped.

In quick succession he launched the first things that came to hand at the landlord; six jugs, two glasses and a poker, which Dawson was forced to parry as best he could. The other customers, including several women, told the attacker to go away, though these were probably not the actual words used. Instead of taking their good advice, the failed bacon vendor laid into them with his boots, severely kicking one unfortunate lady about the shins. The landlord, having armed himself, now sallied into the fray and Farrell finally got his drink, thrown at him by Dawson who subsequently succeeded in evicting him. Humiliated, Farrell fell to his knees and swore vengeance, vowing that he would rip the landlord from head to toe, even if it took him six months to do so.

When Ashton produced the warrant for his arrest, Farrell ran to the roof of the house, and, following what the local paper described as 'an exciting chase', he was captured and sent down for two months.

Being assaulted came as part and parcel of the policeman's lot. Described as 'two rough-looking youths' John Riley and Charles Campbell seemed to hold a grudge against all policemen, having been convicted on nineteen separate occasions, mostly for assaults on the rozzers.

Our intrepid crime stalker, Warrant officer Ashton and one P.C. Howell, who had previously felt the leather of Riley's belt, roused him in his Rochdale Road lair. Despite the early hour, news of the arrest

89. Police frequently came under attack when effecting an arrest, the mob usually trying to knock off their helmets. Prostitutes and drunkards were wont to spit in the face of an arresting officer.

90. *Prostitutes would entice drunken men into dark alleyways with the promise of a knee-trembler. More often than not the victim was set about by a bully or in some cases a female co-operative.*

spread so quickly on the rogue's grapevine that by the time the trio emerged from the house, a group of rent-a-crowd yobbos had assembled threateningly by the doorstep.

"*Give it to 'em!*" screamed Riley. Empty pop bottles began raining down with some accuracy on the two policemen. Ashton's hat was knocked off and Howell fell to the ground clutching his face. With the arrival of reinforcements, the fellow accused in the dock, Campbell, was arrested for having thrown a bottle. The police-hater, Riley, was sent down for 6 months, and police-baiter, Campbell, for 2.

Cases of assault were not all one-way. At times officers would mete out their own form of instant justice. Many youngsters' ears were left ringing following a hefty clip. In one telling statement, reported by the local press, it appears that career criminals were sometimes punished on the spot. When Edward Smith was charged with loitering *he was said to have "begged the officers to kick him and let him go."*

Women would often prey on male victims who were three sheets to the wind. Sometimes they would hunt with a male 'bully', entice the drunkard to follow them down a dark alleyway with the promise of sexual favours, and there relieve him of his valuables. The three Marys dispensed with the bully and set up a female co-operative.

Mary Ann Carney, Mary Smith and Mary Rourk were stopped by Ashton in Angel Meadow as they struggled to relieve the drunken Robert Singleton of cash. All four were arrested, Singleton for being drunk and the three women for attempted robbery. The hapless victim was locked up for the night and fined 5 shillings with costs. On the way to the police station, Ashton saw Mary Smith discard some of the evidence, throwing away a sovereign, which he swiftly recovered from the pavement. With no previous convictions Mary Rourk was warned as to her future behaviour. The other two Marys, being habitual offenders, were sentenced to a month each with hard labour. Smith brazenly asked if she could have her sovereign returned. The clerk was having none of it. 'Tell her to go down,' he snapped.

Edward Norton, described as 'a repulsive-looking character', was charged with living on the improper earnings of what was euphemistically termed an 'unfortunate' woman. Ashton had known Norton for six years, during which time he had never known him to have a job. Norton admitted that his income came through thieving but he vehemently denied being a pimp!

He was sentenced to three years with hard labour.

Patrick Hughes from Gaythorn appeared in court charged with assaulting the wife of the keeper of the Vulcan Inn. Mrs. Lowry testified that on Monday afternoon a gang of youths entered the pub and demanded to be allowed to pass through to the kitchen. When permission was refused, the drunken Hughes picked up a stool and threw it through a window. He then attacked Mrs. Lowry and jumped onto the counter to kick her in the chest.

Hughes had a different version of events. He stated that he simply walked into the Vulcan Inn and politely requested to be allowed to pass through into the kitchen. When told this was not possible he calmly accepted the decision and asked to be served with beer in the vault. For some unknown reason the landlord, without provocation, struck him. He of course had to defend himself and struck just two blows in self-defence. Tears were swelling in his eyes as he insisted he was a wronged man and begged for mercy. No one believed him.

Once a guilty verdict had been arrived at magistrates would often ask policemen what they knew of the alleged offender. Ashton informed the court that Hughes was captain of a gang of scuttlers and a dangerous character. This information led to him spending the next two months toiling at the Crown's expense.

91. Partners in crime.

LAUGHTER IN COURT

If you want to get a drink, ask a Policeman!
He will manage it, I think, will a policeman,
If the pubs are shut or not,
He'll produce the flowing pot,
He can open all the lot, can a Policeman

In 1911 a constable (5th class) on appointment could expect to earn 26 shillings per week; an inspector (1st class) with 12 years service received 60 shillings and a superintendent up to £290 per annum.

The constable's pay could vary every week according to a reward and fine system. Policemen would often be cited for bravery in rescuing people from burning houses or harnessing runaway horses. Rewards varied from 2s.6d. to £1. In lean times it was not unknown for an accomplice to aim a hefty smack on the fetlocks of an unmanned horse and cart and for a constable to miraculously appear and seize the bolting horse in front of an admiring public. On the whole, however, it was more a case of penalties than profit.

Punishments were strict and fines the rule even for minor cases of lateness. Below are a list of penalties meted out in 1911:

NAME	OFFENCE and PENALTY
Walter Spicer	Being off his patrol and gossiping with B213 Cowin in Great Ducie street. **Fine 5s.**
Sgt. Ed. McDermott	Drunk when on special duty at Belle Vue Gardens at 8.25. p.m. 26th December 1910. **Reduced one class**
Jas Hamey	Neglecting to detain and make proper enquiries respecting a man found without shoes and acting in a suspicious manner in Rochdale Road at 12.50. a.m. **Fine 5s.**
Daniel Sweeney	Drunk when on duty in uniform on Stockport Road at 1.50.p.m. **To resign forthwith.**
Thomas Gardiner	Behaving in a manner unbecoming a police officer and paying addresses to a single woman to whom he falsely represented himself as a single man. **To resign forthwith.**
Henry Lee	Breaking and entering a shop at 79, Tamworth street Hulme. **Dismissed.**
Fred Chesters	Failing to find a lockup shop at 458, Oldham road had been broken into at 7.20.a.m. **Fine 5s.**
Thomas Hughes	Riding a bike without a light in Conran street when in uniform at 9.20.p.m. Refusal to stop when attention was drawn by sergeant. **Fine 2s. 6d.**
Sergeant Lewis	Drunk when on duty. **Reduced one class viz 2s. weekly**
George Chilton	Disobedience of orders. Insolence to Acting Sergeant Stanton when ordered to lock up premises. **Fine 10s.**
Frederick Wickenden	Frequenting Cleveland Buildings in Market street for the purpose of obtaining and consuming intoxicating liquor whilst on duty on 3, 4, 5th May 1911. **To forfeit two conduct badges.**
Edward Groarke	Assaulting Albert Rafferty, a prisoner, in the charge office at Whitworth. **One day's leave stopped.**
Richard Pattison	Smoking a wooden pipe whilst on duty in a public place. **Fine 2s.6d.**
Henry Jones	Behaving in a manner unbecoming a police officer by associating with thieves, prostitutes and a betting man. **To resign forthwith.**
Willie Vincent	Gossiping with a fireman at Denmark Road Fire Station for ten minutes. **Fine 2s. 6d.**
John Forrest	Behaving in a disrespectful and insolent manner to Inspector Brassington in Goulden Street Station. **Fine 2s. 6d.**

92. A spot inspection interrupts routine police questioning outside London Road fire station?

G Quayle — Irregularly working his beat and being sat down with his helmet off in a coal yard in Nelson Place. **Fine 5s.**

George Hamilton — Neglecting to wear white gloves when on duty and using insolent language to his inspector when spoken to respecting his dirty uniform. **One day's leave stopped.**

T Fitton — Neglecting to work his beat from 1.35 to 1.45 a.m. and being in the dwelling house occupied by a widow named Emma Read. **Fine 10s.**

Thomas Chapman — Behaving in a manner unbecoming a police officer by systematically frequenting and drinking in certain public houses and associating with undesirable people. Also frequently quarrelling with his wife and assaulting her on 22nd June 1911. **Punishment not recorded.**

Thomas Keogh — Being found asleep on a sofa in the house 64, Midland street, Ardwick, occupied by Mary Hughes. **Fine 10s.**

James Jack Proby — Visiting the dwelling house at 70, Higher Ardwick for an improper purpose. **To resign forthwith.**

Thomas Coverdale — Neglecting to work his beat for 15 minutes from 3. 25 to 3.40. a.m. and being seated on a window sill smoking and gossiping with D199 Copley. **Fine 2s.6d.**

Arthur J Wyatt — Visiting the Albert hotel, Quay street when off duty; also consulting with a prostitute. **To resign forthwith.**

Thomas Griffin — Wasting his time and being sat down in a room at Mill Street Station for one hour, 15 minutes when on duty. **Two hours extra duty.**

FOND OF A DRINK

Martin Cleary, the man who appeared in the dock at the Manchester Police court on Saturday, garbed in a sack stepped up again this morning in the same attire. He was arrested for two petty thefts, Detective-sergeant Ashton and Detective Winter noticing him in Dantzic street on Friday night apparently hiding articles under his coat. While in the cells that night Cleary tore his suit to tatters.

After the evidence this morning the presiding magistrate queried: 'I suppose you are fond of a drink.' Cleary was much surprised. He bent forward with eagerness, and expectantly replied: 'Yes, Sir'. Then he saw he had made a mistake. Sentence of two months imprisonment was passed.

Throughout his career William Ashton encountered all manner of rogues, bullies, brutes, burglars, drunkards, pimps, prostitutes and wife-beaters. They ranged in intelligence from the sophisticated fraudster to the illiterate shoplifter.

None can have been as soft as a young Mancunian, whose crass stupidity almost beggars belief. The following story was reported in the local press in the early 1900s.

A young man named Fred Hobson the other night walked into the Detective Office at the Manchester Town Hall and inquired from Detective Inspector Ashton whether there was a warrant out for his arrest. The officer asked what it might be for, and Hobson replied that it was for stealing £70 eight years ago. The officer looked up the records, and finding that there was such a warrant out told Hobson so.

'Has it been renewed?' asked the young man.

'No,' replied the officer; 'it does not require renewal.'

'Oh, I thought it did,' observed Hobson who a few minutes later found himself under arrest.

Hobson had no choice. He served four months hard labour for his curiosity

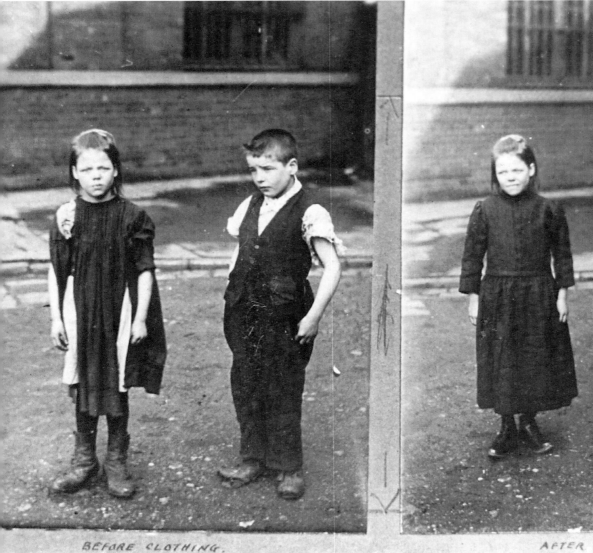

BEFORE CLOTHING.

AFTER CLOTHING.

93. Police would do what they could to help clothe street waifs. You certainly couldn't accuse the girl in the left picture of being too big for her boots!

232

Rebecca Fineberg

a Jewish Prostitute

Her modus Operandi is to entice men into a house get them to undress and go to bed whilst the man is in bed one of Bullies rifles his pockets - known on B. Division

94. As to B Division: was this in the Biblical sense?

DROWNING HIS SORROWS...

When Paddy's mother died his sole thoughts were as to how he could profit from the bereavement. Mrs. Walsh's life had been blighted by her son's 28 convictions and he was awaiting trial for breaking and entering when news of her death reached him.

Not one to miss a golden opportunity, Paddy pleaded with the magistrate to release him so he could organise the funeral, not wanting his mother to be buried as a pauper by the Chorlton Guardians. He promised the authorities that he would turn over a new leaf once he got her *'in the clay'*.

Paddy was released and promptly organised a collection from both the neighbours and his mother's friends, to pay the funeral costs. Nine days after her death, the remains of Mrs. Walsh were still awaiting burial. Paddy spent all the money getting blind drunk. He eventually contacted the Guardians to dispose of the body. Paddy appeared in court with the self-satisfied, smug smile of an inebriate as he was sent down for two months.

DESTINATION DARTMOOR

Edward Monaghan was on his last legs. At 61, and with no settled address, all he wanted was some rest and a square meal. There was only one place he was certain would provide for him. Following his arrest for smashing the window of Samuel Withnall's jewellery shop at 55, Oxford Road, Edwards willingly confessed adding that he didn't want to be *'like many fellows, lousy and dirty, knocking about lodging-houses; I'd rather go back to Dartmoor. We now have a good Home Secretary.'*

In a preliminary hearing, Edward seemed quite proud of his actions:

'I smashed the window too high. I should have hit the window lower and then I could have cleared it. There was a chap on a bicycle passing when I broke the window. He was coming to speak to me, but I went like that (shaking his fist) and he went off (laughter in court). I had two pals with me. I put them at the corner, but as soon as I broke the window they bolted off.' (Loud laughter).

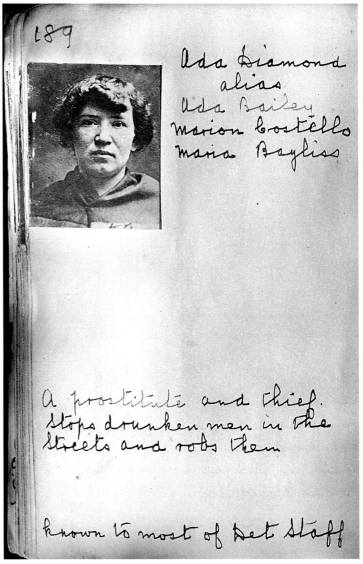

189

Ada Diamond alias Ada Bailey Marion Costello Maria Bayliss

a prostitute and thief. Stops drunken men in the streets and robs them

known to most of Det Staff

95. What inferences should we make about the conduct of detectives in relation to Ada Diamond?

Henry Street

A Bogus Tea Company. Fraud.

His "modus Operandi" is to call upon people and represent that if they buy a lb of tea at the end of the month they get a Bonus of 20/-

known to a Sergeant Chidley

96. There's one born every minute.

MERRY CHRISTMAS, YOUR HONOUR

Some career criminals looked upon gaol as being no more than an occupational hazard. Edward Armstrong, who was arrested by Ashton for stealing from a shop till, changed his plea of guilty to one of innocent when he learned that he had to go to the sessions for trial.

At trial, having forgotten his amended plea, Edward corrected a witness who'd stated that £3 had been stolen from the shop – the real amount, Armstrong pointed out, had been a little less than that! He later denied ever having been near the fish shop in Rochdale Road where the theft took place.

Feeling that he had gotten off lightly, even though he was of course innocent, Edward greeted his sentence of three months by wishing Mr. Brierley a Merry Christmas and a Happy New Year.

Two other prisoners, Sarah Ann Asker and Harry Wilson, seemed positively pleased with the lightness of their sentences of two and three months. They had been found guilty of stealing a purse containing a half sovereign, a guinea and a breast-pin. Sarah Ann left the dock laughing and Harry picked up his hat, and lifted it and aimed a joyous kick at its crown

A MARKED CARD

Throughout the 1800s fortune-tellers were dragged before the courts charged with obtaining money by false pretences. Police would stake out their premises and sometimes send in a plain clothes officer or female volunteer.

In the 1870s Elizabeth Hodgson appeared before the court. A few days previously Kate Dunn, under the supervision of Police-constable Kelsall, visited the middle-aged soothsayer. Elizabeth had not seen her coming and she was one of thirteen visitors that day.

It appears that Elizabeth was not the most patient of soothsayers, as Kate's testimony revealed. After shuffling a pack of cards Elizabeth asked whether her visitor knew *a dark woman*. She then shuffled the cards again and inquired as to whether Kate knew *a dark-complexioned man*. Kate replied that she did not. Elizabeth's reply brought about much laughter in court:

"You are a lying _____, you do."

Elizabeth had no need of a crystal ball or cards to know where she would spend the next two months.

A VICIOUS-LOOKING VIXEN

Mary Ann Cavanagh, unflatteringly described in the local press as a *vicious-looking vixen*, was one of many appearing before the courts following disruption in a workhouse.

In March 1864 Mary took it upon herself to brighten up the normally dull routine of Sunday morning. In the recreation yard she entertained her fellow paupers with a rendering of the most '*filthy and immoral*' songs learned by heart after spending many years in bawdy taverns. This behaviour on the sabbath was, naturally, not greatly appreciated by workhouse officials. Mary's crime, however, was compounded that very evening when she attacked the superintendent, a Miss Swallow. The vixen became extremely vicious, punching Miss Swallow in the face and attempting to remove the hair from her head by the roots.

In court Mary continuously interrupted proceedings with cries of : *"Eh, what lies!"* and *"I wonder you are not ashamed, telling stories there; you know it is all a lie."* When sentenced to a month's imprisonment she threatened revenge on Bridget Hogan, one of the witnesses: *"I'll have it out of you Hogan, when I get back again."*

97. The first stop on the way to the courts.

EQUALITY BEFORE THE LAW

John Kennedy and his wife Alice were arrested for waylaying drunken men with the intention of robbing them. John was sentenced to three months and his wife, two. Incensed at not being treated equally Alice demanded that the judge give her an extra month. This was refused but Alice was back in the dock again two minutes later charged with breaking two plate glass windows in the property office of the courthouse after striking them with her fist. She had left the dock swearing and cursing everybody within earshot but when she returned had a perceptible smile on her lips.

Mr. Brierley: *"What did you do it for?"*

Alice Kennedy: *"What did I do it for? Why do people make false statements? I got my two months for nothing. I don't intend to do another for nothing."*

Mr. Brierley: *"You must go to gaol for a further month."*

Having achieved her aim Alice flashed a rare smile of triumph to the baffled court officials.

DRUNK ON TEA

When reading through old newspapers it's very easy to get side-tracked by intriguing headlines. This story dates from 1867 and centres round Mary Ann Maguire, a plain speaking, no nonsense sort of woman charged with being drunk and disorderly. She told the magistrate that she had not been drunk for three months having taken the pledge on 1st. May. She admitted that if she had had the chance she would have broken the pledge and insisted that she would never be a teetotaller again for three months if she could get drink. Her problem was that she simply had no money and her husband refused to hand over any of his earnings. Mary was questioned by the magistrate:

Mr. Trafford: *"Were you drunk on Saturday?"*

Mary: *"No."*

Mr. Trafford: *"Do you mean to say that you had nothing to drink on Saturday? Nothing to drink? No gin?"*

Mary: *"I never drink gin at all; it's whiskey I drink " (laughter)*

Mr. Trafford: *"Well, how much whiskey had you?"*

Mary: *"I had no whiskey; he would not give me any money. I had nothing but tea on Saturday."*

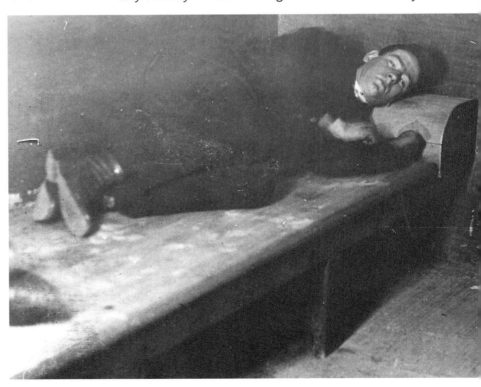

98. An interesting, if uncomfortable cell. The foot on the left side indicates it's a double-room.

1. Site of the New Bayley Prison which saw 6 men publicly hanged in the 1860s.

2. Strangeways. Of the 44 executed before 1914, 42 were male.

3. Deansgate had such a reputation for debauchery and general low life that one writer recommended it be renamed Devil's Gate.

4. Charter Street. Referring to the numerous lodging houses in 1870s *'It is all free fighting here, even some of the windows do not open so it is useless to cry for help.'*

5. The floor of the privies in Style Street in the 1870s was described as *'a flood of urine and a puss of ordure.'*

6. Barrow Street, Salford. The cellar of No. 31 was home to 18 people. In the back cellar Thomas Andrews, his wife and six children slept on the floor in two beds of shavings.

7. Wood Street pub in 1870s. *'The women were all bareheaded save the strata of cheap oil and the dust of weeks which covered their hair'*.

8. The pubs in Oxford Street were said to house *'one mass of prostitute, thief and fool.'*

9. Back Piccadilly. The very bottom end of the prostitute market. Here were eight houses for women *'too young, too old or too ugly'* to walk the streets and the destination of similar men.

10. Canal Street 1870s. *'The women are of a class whose degradation is utter, and whose reclamation, as a body, is an absolute impossibility'*.

11. Nelson Street, where Caminada set out to trap a group of quacks masquerading as doctors.

12. The Hidden Gem Church. Caminada would sit in the back pews and hear 'confession' from his snouts.

13. Garfield Street. Scene of the Salford tragedy of 1888 where Samuel Derby murdered his wife and six children and then took his own life.

14. George Ellis pushed his wife through an upstairs window in William Street. He was hanged in 1871.

15. William Walsh threw his 16-year-old sweetheart into the river Medlock (1888).

16. Mary Wilson threw herself in the canal near Minshull Street. She could not afford to live on a weekly wage of 2s. 2d. in 1888. She was rescued by a dog.

17. Hyde Road. 1875. Margaret McKivett died from the effects of a botched abortion. Despite the jury's recommendation for mercy Alfred Heap was hanged in Liverpool. His last words: *'Receive my soul'*.

18. The remains of a murdered baby were found in a pail in Red Bank, 1888. Such discoveries barely merited more than a few lines in the local newspaper.

19. Victoria Station. In 1865 Mary Bibby murdered her own baby, wrapped her in a parcel and sent it to Preston. She wanted to find work in domestic service and the presence of her young daughter prevented this.

20. Greater Manchester Police Museum. An Aladdin's cave for researchers and students. Open to the public on Tuesdays.

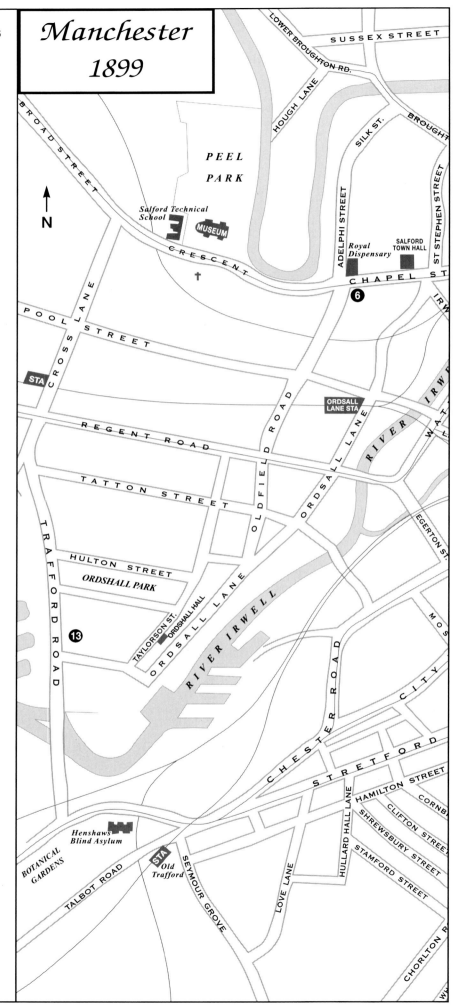

Manchester 1899

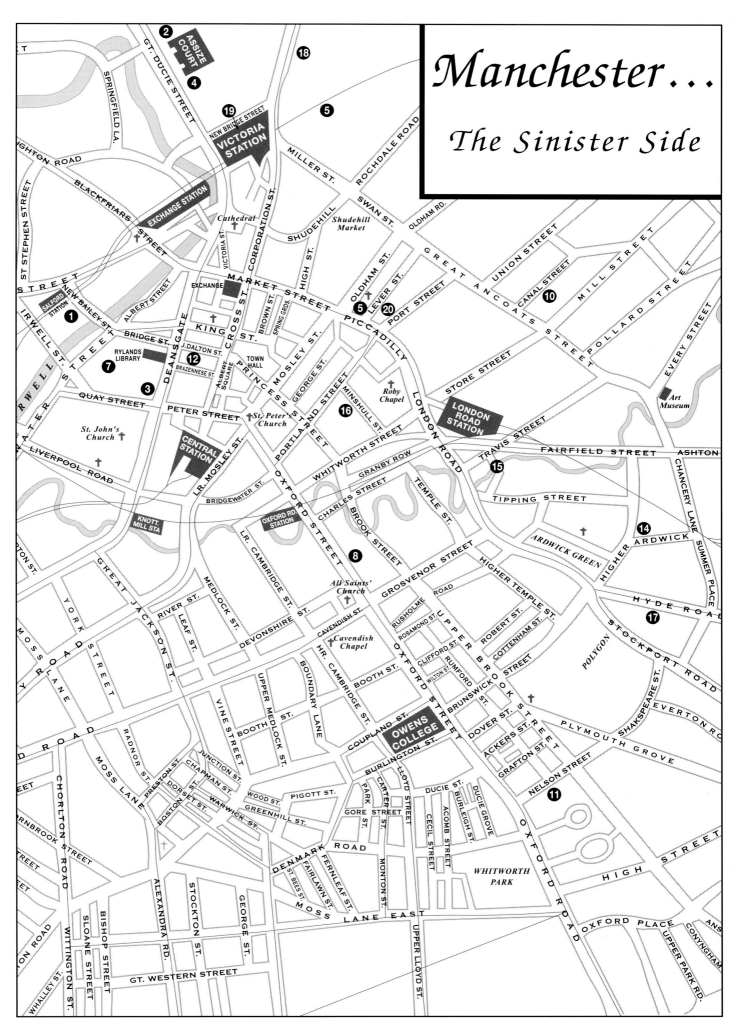

Manchester...

The Sinister Side

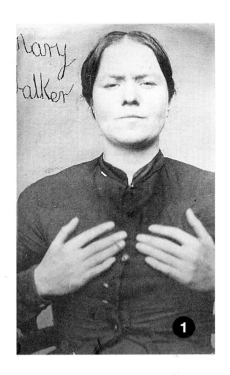

THE SAME BUT DIFFERENT?

The problems of identification faced by police (and this photo researcher) were compounded by the frequent use of pseudonyms. Prisoners with previous convictions were likely to receive higher sentences, so anonymity was sought by all. During the course of research I came across newspaper reports of four women who may or may not be related, or indeed the same person! We cannot trust the names they gave to arresting officers, so let's call them Nos. 1, 2, 3 and 4.

No. 1 was entered in the police record book as Mary Walker, alias **Ann Kelly.** Her first conviction, in 1876, was for being a rogue and thief. She served several sentences for prostitution, larceny and being a rogue and vagabond.

No. 2 is **Annie Kelly,** allegedly 58 years old with over 69 prosecutions for drunkenness, indecent exposure and prostitution. The photo was taken in 1923.

No. 3, who looks very similar to No. 1, gave her profession as waste sorter; her name as Julia McHale, alias Robinson, alias **Hartley.** She specialised in stealing shawls and coats. She received several lengthy sentences in the 1860s and 70s. Miss McHale was entered in the records as being 28 in 1876.

No. 4 Taken in 1917 is Elizabeth Davies, alias Ann Stow, Ann Charlton, Ann McCormack and Mary Jane **Hartley.** She owned up to being 65 in 1917. The police records reveal a long list of convictions for larceny from the person etc.

Probably four entirely different people, but then again...

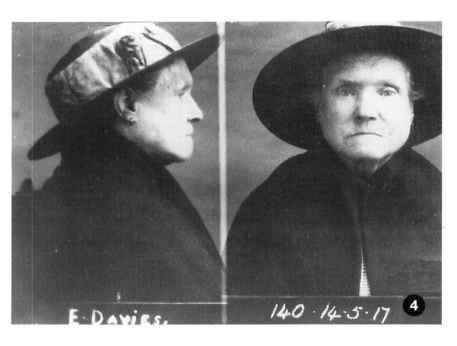

Here ends the trip back in time to Victorian Manchester. If there is sufficient demand, a second book, with similar tales from 1914 onwards, will be in the shops before too long.

I hope you enjoyed a 'wicked read.'

STEVE JONES,
Nottingham, June 1997.